Pita Breads and Pocket Fillings

by
Darcy Williamson and John Allgair

Photo cover by John Allgair

Copyright © 1981 Darcy Williamson and John Allgair

All rights reserved. No part of the material protected by this copyright notice may be reproduced or utilized in any form or by any means, electronic or mechanical, including photocopying, recording, or by any informational storage and retrieval system without written permission from the copyright owner. Printed in the United States of America.

Dedicated to Eve

CONTENTS

Chapter 1 Basic Pita and Fillings 3
Chapter 2 Cornmeal Pita and Fillings 14
Chapter 3 Rye Pita and Fillings 24
Chapter 4 Sesame Pita and Fillings 34
Chapter 5 Sourdough Pita and Fillings 46
Chapter 6 Triticale Pita and Fillings 62
Chapter 7 Whole Wheat Pita and Fillings 72
Chapter 8 Hors d'Oeuvre Pita Fillings 83
Chapter 9 Dessert Pita and Fillings 92
Chapter 10 More Cold Fillings 104
Chapter 11 More Hot Fillings 116
Index 127

INTRODUCTION

One afternoon I planned an impromptu picnic. By impromptu, I mean I was driving past a park, noticed an abundance of individuals digging into brown paper sacks and white McDonalds bags and realized that it was lunch time. I stopped at a nearby shopping center and, being in one of my adventurous moods, bought my first pita bread (they were on sale). After a quick stop at the supermarket deli, I was off to the park. I cut the pita in half and started filling the pockets with corned beef, Swiss cheese, and cole-slaw. I won't shame myself by telling how many stuffed pockets I ate that afternoon. My theory that the Lebanese, Arabs, Greeks, and other foreign folk had eaten pita for centuries because they didn't have access to hamburger buns, hogie rolls, and ready-made taco shells, no longer seemed valid. I was suddenly hooked on pita and found I prefered them to any of the above mentioned.

There are thousands of other pita enthusiasts. Sandwich shops, restaurants and commercial airlines are serving it. It's being featured in natural food stores and the bakery sections of supermarkets. John and I discovered a sandwich shop in Whitefish, Montana, which served all their sandwich fillings in pita pockets.

Pita deserves its notoriety. It's not only nutritious, it's simple to bake. Since the foods I most enjoy cooking are those which appear to be difficult, but aren't, pita and I became quick partners in the kitchen. I had so much fun making pita that John got his fifteen year old sourdough starter out and started making his own sourdough versions. Within an hour of beginning, pita bread is baked and ready to fill. Several dozen pitas can be baked within a couple of hours. Since this bread doesn't stay fresh long, those not used within a day or two should be frozen. To freshen the frozen bread to "just baked" flavor and texture, place them on a cookie sheet and heat in a preheated 450°F. oven for two to three minutes.

Pita is also a versatile bread. Have you ever filled a sandwich with lots of gooey fillings, topped it with guacamole AND sour cream and eaten it out of hand without the filling ending in your lap? Pita is filled with all sorts of gooey, messy fillings and eaten with success as long as one basic rule is followed: Fill pockets just before serving.

Once you get involved in making your own pita, you may wish to share your talent with friends by throwing a pita party. The pitas can be baked in advance and frozen. Fillings can also be prepared ahead of time and reheated prior to serving or kept warm in a chafing dish. Let guests fill their own pockets (pita) with various fillings. The feast is on!

Chapter 1

Basic Pita and Fillings

BASIC PITA

1½ cups lukewarm water
1 pkg. active dry yeast
2 tsp. sugar
½ tsp. salt
3½ cups all-purpose flour

    Place yeast and sugar in large bowl. Add water and stir carefully to blend. Set aside in warm place until frothy (approximately 10 minutes). Stir in salt and flour, then turn onto floured board and knead for about 10 minutes. Divide dough into 12 balls and roll the balls into 6" rounds, ⅛" thick.

    Place rounds on lightly greased cookie sheets, cover with damp cloth and let rise in warm place for 40 to 45 minutes. Meanwhile preheat oven to 500°F.

    Bake bread in preheated oven for 5 to 7 minutes or until lightly browned. Makes 1 dozen.

AUSTRIAN BEEF FILLING (4 servings)

1 lb. steak, cut into thin strips
1 onion, sliced
1 Tbsp. tomato sauce
1 clove garlic, minced
Dash marjoram
½ tsp. caraway seeds
½ tsp. salt
¼ tsp. pepper
3 Tbsp. margarine
½ head red cabbage
2 basic pitas, halved

Combine steak with onion, tomato sauce, garlic, and seasonings. Sauté in margarine a few minutes, then add cabbage and sauté a few minutes longer. Fill pockets and serve at once.

AVOCADO-HAM SCRAMBLE (4 servings)

1 small avocado, peeled, pitted, and diced
2 tsp. lemon juice
6 eggs
6 Tbsp. cream
½ tsp. salt
¼ tsp. pepper
3 Tbsp. margarine
1 4½-oz. can deviled ham
2 basic pitas, halved

Toss avocado with lemon juice.

Beat together eggs, cream, salt, and pepper. Pour into skillet in which margarine has been melted. When eggs begin to thicken, spoon the deviled ham over. When eggs are done, fold in avocado. Fill pockets and serve immediately.

AVOCADO SALAD IN A PITA (6 servings)

1 cup sliced radishes
3 large ripe avocados, peeled, pitted, and sliced
½ cup diced celery
3 Tbsp. olive oil
2 Tbsp. lemon juice
¼ tsp. salt
¼ tsp. pepper
3 basic pitas, halved

Combine radishes, avocado, and celery. Mix together olive oil, lemon juice, salt and pepper. Toss with avocado mixture. Fill pockets.

DEVILED CHICKEN LIVERS IN POCKETS (4 servings)

1 lb. chicken livers
3 Tbsp. margarine, melted
⅔ cup fine cracker crumbs
2 tsp. margarine
½ tsp. onion powder
Dash cayenne
2 Tbsp. Dijon style mustard
1 Tbsp. catsup
2 tsp. Worcestershire sauce
2 pita rounds, halved

Dip livers in 3 Tbsp. melted margarine; coat with cracker crumbs. Place coated livers on greased cookie sheet and broil 6" from heat for 3 minutes on each side.

Melt 2 tsp. margarine in skillet; stir in onion powder, cayenne, mustard, catsup, and Worcestershire sauce. Heat to boiling.

Fill pockets with broiled livers and spoon sauce over. Serve at once.

FRANK IN A POCKET (4 servings)

4 dinner franks
3 Tbsp. margarine
2 basic pitas, halved
Mustard
Catsup
Hot dog relish
Diced onions

Sauté franks in margarine until well cooked. Put a frank in each pocket and top with desired topping.

FRENCH TENDERLOIN FILLING (4 servings)

1 lb. beef tenderloin, cut into thin strips
¼ cup tarragon vinegar
⅛ tsp. thyme
⅛ tsp. nutmeg
⅛ tsp. ground cloves
Bay leaf
½ onion, sliced thin
¼ lemon, sliced thin
½ tsp. salt
2 pitas, halved

Combine meat strips with remaining ingredients (except pita) and marinate 3 hours or longer.

Remove bay leaf and lemon. Stir-fry beef in marinade to desired doneness. Fill pockets, using slotted spoon.

GREEK BEEF POCKETS (4 servings)

3/4 lb. ground beef
1 medium onion, diced
3/4 cup water
2 Tbsp. flour
1/2 tsp. salt
3/4 tsp. oregano leaves
1/4 tsp. pepper
1 medium tomato, diced
1/2 cup sliced, pitted black olives
2 Tbsp. red wine vinegar
1/4 lb. feta cheese, crumbled
2 basic pitas, halved

Cook beef and onion in skillet until meat is cooked. Drain fat. Combine flour and water. Stir into meat mixture, along with salt, oregano, and pepper. Heat to boiling. Remove from heat and stir in tomato, olives, vinegar and cheese. Fill pockets with mixture.

HASH IN A POCKET (4 servings)

2 medium potatoes, boiled, peeled, and diced
1 Tbsp. butter
1/4 cup minced onion
1 Tbsp. minced celery
1 Tbsp. minced green pepper
1/4 tsp. minced garlic
1 1/2 cups diced leftover cooked meat
1/4 cup meat stock
Salt and pepper to taste
2 basic pitas, halved
Chili sauce

Sauté onion, celery, green pepper, and garlic in butter. Add potatoes, meat, stock, salt, and pepper. Cook until heated through. Fill pockets with mixture and serve with chili sauce.

HOT DOGS WITH CHILI BEEF SAUCE (6 servings)

6 frankfurters
1 lb. ground beef
2 cups tomato sauce
1 pkg. prepared chili mix
1 cup chopped onions
3 pitas, halved

Brown meat in skillet. Add tomato sauce and chili mix. Bring to boil and simmer 15 minutes. Meanwhile, broil frankfurters in oven or over hot coals. Place broiled frankfurters in pockets and spoon chili beef sauce over. Top with chopped onions.

LOBSTER SALAD POCKET (4 servings)

1½ cups cooked lobster
3 Tbsp. lemon juice
¾ cup sliced celery
⅓ cup mayonnaise
¼ tsp. salt
2 avocado, peeled and diced
2 basic pitas, halved

Combine first six ingredients in mixing bowl. Chill. Spoon into pockets.

ORIENTAL SCRAMBLE IN A POCKET (4 servings)

8 eggs
1/4 cup sliced sauteed mushrooms
1/2 cup diced cooked pork
1/2 cup drained, sliced bamboo shoots
1 1/2 tsp. soy sauce
3 Tbsp. margarine
2 basic pitas, halved

Beat together eggs, mushrooms, pork, bamboo shoots, and soy sauce. Melt margarine in skillet. Cook as scrambled eggs. Fill pockets with scrambled mixture. Serve with additional soy sauce, if desired.

PITA BEAN BURRITOS (4 servings)

1 1-lb. can refried beans
1 clove garlic, minced
1 onion, chopped
1/2 cup tomato sauce
1 Tbsp. Worcestershire sauce
1 tsp. chili powder
1 tsp. cumin
Few drops hot pepper sauce
Grated cheese
Chopped onion
Shredded lettuce
Taco sauce
2 pitas, halved

Heat beans with garlic, chopped onion, tomato sauce, Worcestershire sauce, chili powder, cumin, and hot pepper sauce. Fill pita pockets with bean mixture, cheese, onion, lettuce, and taco sauce.

PITA KRAUT DOG (8 servings)

1 lb. drained sauerkraut
1 tsp. caraway seeds
1 cup sauteed onion
6 cups flat beer
8 frankfurters
4 pitas, halved
Mustard

In skillet, heat together sauerkraut, caraway seeds, and onion. Meanwhile, boil frankfurters in beer until cooked. Spread mustard on the inside of pockets, add cooked frankfurters and top with sauerkraut mixture.

PITA WITH PARMESAN PATTIES (6 servings)

1½ lbs. ground beef
1 egg, well beaten
1 medium onion, chopped
½ tsp. salt
½ tsp. monosodium glutamate
⅛ tsp. pepper
¾ cup (6-oz. can) tomato paste
1 Tbsp. grated Parmesan cheese
6 slices Mozzarella cheese
3 basic pitas, halved

Mix together beef, egg, onion, and seasoning. Shape meat mixture into a large square ¾" thick. Cut into 6 equal portions.

Broil meat 2" from heat source for 10 minutes. Combine tomato paste with Parmesan cheese. Turn meat and spread on tomato mixture. Top each with Mozzarella and broil until cheese is melted and lightly browned. Slip a patty into each pocket.

POACHED SALMON IN A PITA (4 servings)

4 salmon steaks, 1" thick
1 quart of chicken broth
1 tsp. lemon juice
¼ tsp. salt
1 stalk celery, diced
3 sprigs parsley
1 bay leaf
2 basic pitas, halved
1 lemon, cut into wedges

Combine broth, lemon juice, salt, celery, parsley, and bay leaf in kettle. Bring to boiling. Tie salmon in a square of cheesecloth and submerge in broth. Cover and simmer 10 to 12 minutes. Cool. Chill. Remove any bones or skin from salmon steaks and fill pockets with fish. Squeeze lemon juice over filling.

POCKET OF MEAT LOAF (6 servings)

⅓ cup fine dry bread crumbs
1 cup milk
1 small onion, minced
1½ tsp. margarine
1 lb. ground beef
1 carrot, grated
1 egg
½ tsp. salt
¼ tsp. pepper
½ tsp. ginger
½ tsp. curry powder
3 basic pitas, halved
Chili sauce

Mix together crumbs and milk in mixing bowl. Sauté onion in margarine. Add onion and remaining ingredients (except pita and chili sauce). Shape into loaf. Bake in 350°F. oven 60 minutes. Cool; then chill.
Fill pockets with sliced meat loaf. Top with chili sauce.

POCKET OF PIZZA (8 servings)

½ lb. sliced pepperoni
¼ lb. sliced Canadian bacon, halved
¼ lb. sliced mushrooms
1 6-oz. can tomato paste
⅓ cup grated Parmesan cheese
¼ cup finely chopped onions
¼ cup finely chopped pitted olives
1 tsp. Italian seasoning
3 tomatoes, peeled and diced
1½ cups grated Mozzarella cheese
4 basic pitas, halved

Combine first nine ingredients in saucepan. Heat slowly until heated through. Spoon into pockets, sprinkle cheese over top, stand filled pockets upright in loaf pan and broil until cheese melts.

SALMON-TOMATO FILLING (4 servings)

¼ cup butter
¼ tsp. garlic powder
1 medium tomato, cut into 4 slices
1½ cup flaked salmon
6 Tbsp. chopped sweet pickle
6 Tbsp. sour cream
¼ tsp. salt
⅛ tsp. pepper
2 basic pitas, halved

Combine butter with garlic powder and spread on insides of pockets. Place tomato slice in each pocket.
Combine salmon, pickle, sour cream, salt, and pepper. Divide salmon mixture among pockets. Stand pockets upright in loaf pan and broil until filling is hot and bubbling.

SLOPPY JOE'S IN PITA (6 servings)

1 Tbsp. oil
½ cup chopped onion
½ cup chopped green pepper
1 ¼ lb. ground beef
2 cups tomato sauce
2 Tbsp. bottled chili sauce
2 tsp. Worcestershire sauce
3 basic pitas, halved

Heat oil in skillet and cook onion, green pepper, and ground beef, breaking up beef with fork, until beef is browned. Drain off fat. Add tomato sauce, chili sauce, and Worcestershire. Stir well and heat through. Spoon into pockets and serve immediately.

SWEET-SOUR VEAL FILLING (6 servings)

1 20½-oz. can pineapple tidbits
1 ½ lb. veal, cut into 1 ½" cubes
2 Tbsp. salad oil
½ cup chopped onion
¼ tsp. salt
⅛ tsp. pepper
1 beef bouillon cube
1 cup boiling water
1 cup diced celery
3 Tbsp. cornstarch
3 Tbsp. soy sauce
2 Tbsp. vinegar
1 3-oz. can sliced mushrooms, drained
3 basic pitas, halved

Drain pineapple, reserving syrup. Brown veal in hot oil. Add onion, salt, pepper, and syrup. Dissolve bouillon in boiling water; pour over meat. Cover and simmer 50 minutes. Add celery and cook 10 minutes longer. Mix cornstarch with soy sauce and vinegar. Stir into hot mixture. Cook until thickened and bubbly. Add pineapple and mushrooms. Heat. Spoon into pockets.

Chapter 2

Cornmeal Pita and Fillings

CORNMEAL PITA

1½ cups lukewarm water
1 pkg. active dry yeast
1 Tbsp. sugar
½ tsp. salt
2½ cups all-purpose flour
1 cup cornmeal

    Add yeast and sugar to lukewarm water and set aside in warm place until mixture becomes frothy. Stir in salt, flour, and cornmeal. Turn onto cornmeal and floured board and knead for 10 minutes. Divide dough into 12 balls and roll each into a 6" round, ⅛" thick. Place rounds on lightly greased cookie or baking sheets, cover with damp cloth and let rise in warm place for 45 minutes.
    Bake in preheated 500°F. oven for 6 to 8 minutes. Makes 1 dozen.

BEEF-RAISIN FILLING (2 servings)

2 cups minced cooked beef
½ cup seedless raisins
½ cup blanched slivered almonds
Bay leaf
Dash cumin
Dash oregano
1 cup red wine
1 cornmeal pita, halved

Combine all ingredients (except pita) and simmer in skillet until most of the wine has evaporated. Remove bay leaf and fill pockets with beef mixture.

CALIFORNIA ENERGY FILLING (2 servings)

½ cup peanut butter
2 slices Monterey Jack cheese
½ cup Mung bean sprouts
½ avocado, sliced
1 cornmeal pita, halved

Spread peanut butter in pockets. Cut cheese into 6 pieces and place three in each pocket. Top with sprouts and avocado slices.

CHILI BURGER IN A CORNMEAL POCKET (6 servings)

1 lb. ground beef
½ cup shredded lettuce
1 cup grated Cheddar cheese
¼ cup chopped Bermuda onion
1 cup chopped onion
1 clove garlic, minced
1½ Tbsp. chili powder
1 can (1-lb.) red kidney beans, drained
1 can (1-lb.) tomatoes, drained
1 small can tomato paste
Few drops hot pepper sauce
3 cornmeal pitas, halved

Shape beef into 6 patties and set aside.

Make chili sauce by combining 1 cup chopped onion, garlic, chili powder, kidney beans, tomatoes, tomato paste, and hot pepper sauce in saucepan. Bring ingredients to boiling, reduce heat, and simmer 30 minutes, stirring occasionally.

Fry hamburger patties in skillet. Place a cooked patty in each pocket. Top with chili mixture, lettuce, grated cheese, and onion. Serve at once.

CHORIZO-FRIJOLE FILLING (4 servings)

3 chorizos
2 cups refried beans
2 cups shredded lettuce
¼ cup minced onion
½ cup guacamole or mashed avocado
½ cup shredded Cheddar cheese
2 cornmeal pitas, halved
Hot sauce

Skin and finely chop chorizos; brown in skillet. Heat refried beans. Spread ½ cup heated beans in inside of each pocket; add sausage, shredded lettuce, onion, guacamole, and cheese. Pass the hot sauce.

FLOUNDER IN A POCKET (6 servings)

1 16-oz. pkg. frozen flounder fillets
8 radishes, finely shredded
2 medium carrots, finely shredded
1 small zucchini, finely shredded
1 Tbsp. vinegar
3 tsp. sugar
Salad oil
1½ tsp. salt
¼ tsp. pepper
1 cup dried bread crumbs
¼ cup milk
3 cornmeal pitas, halved

Thaw fish slightly.
Combine radishes, carrots, zucchini, vinegar, sugar, 3 Tbsp. salad oil, 1 tsp. salt, and pepper in medium bowl. Set aside and stir frequently.
Mix together bread crumbs and ½ tsp. salt. Divide fish into 6 portions. Dip each portion in milk, then roll in bread crumbs. Cook fish in ¼ cup hot oil in skillet 5 to 7 minutes.
Place fillets in pita pockets and top with vegetable mixture. Serve at once.

FRANK OLÉ (8 servings)

8 frankfurters
1 16-oz. can refried beans
1 cup shredded Cheddar cheese
2 cups shredded lettuce
Taco sauce
4 cornmeal pitas, halved

In skillet, over medium heat, cook frankfurters until browned. In saucepan, heat beans.
Spread warmed beans on inside of pockets. Add cheese, frankfurters, lettuce, and taco sauce to taste.

HUEVOS ESPANOL EN UN BOLSILLO (2 servings)

1 canned mild green chili, diced
1 green onion, sliced
2 Tbsp. diced green pepper
1/4 cup diced tomato
3 Tbsp. margarine
2 large eggs
2 Tbsp. milk
1/4 tsp. salt
1 Tbsp. taco sauce
1/4 cup grated sharp Cheddar cheese
1 cornmeal pita, halved
Hot salsa

Melt margarine in skillet; add vegetables and sauté. Combine eggs, milk, salt, and taco sauce. Scramble in lightly oiled skillet. Fold in sauteed vegetables. Fill pockets; lay on a baking sheet and sprinkle with cheese. Broil until cheese melts. Serve at once with salsa.

PITA ENCHILADA (8 servings)

1 lb. ground beef, crumbled
1 15-oz. can kidney beans
1 Tbsp. chili powder
1/4 tsp. salt
3 Tbsp. cooking oil
2 cloves garlic, minced
1 cup chopped onion
2 Tbsp. flour
2 1/2 cups tomato puree
1/4 cup chopped green chilies
1/2 tsp. cumin
2 cups grated Cheddar cheese
4 cornmeal pitas, halved

Brown meat in skillet. Drain fat. Add kidney beans, chili powder,

and salt. Mix well. Set aside. Keep warm.
Heat 3 Tbsp. oil in skillet and sauté garlic and onion. Stir in flour, tomato puree, chilies, and cumin. Simmer 10 minutes.

Place meat mixture in pockets, spoon over sauce and sprinkle with cheese. Stand pockets upright in loaf pan and broil until cheese melts.

Variations: Whole-kernel corn, diced black olives, or minced green pepper can be added to meat mixture.

POCKET FULL OF CHILI (6 servings)

1 lb. ground beef
2 medium onions, diced
3 cloves garlic, minced
1 medium green pepper, diced
¼ cup chili powder (less for milder chili)
1 16-oz. can tomatoes
½ 6-oz. can tomato paste
1 Tbsp. packed brown sugar
1 tsp. oregano leaves
¼ tsp. paprika
1 16-oz. can red kidney beans, drained
3 cornmeal pitas, halved
Grated Cheddar cheese

In large skillet, cook beef, onion, garlic, and green pepper until meat is browned. Drain fat. Add chili powder and cook 1 minute.

Stir in tomatoes, tomato paste, brown sugar, oregano, and paprika. Heat to boiling, stirring to break up tomatoes. Reduce heat, cover and simmer gently 45 minutes, stirring occasionally.

Stir in beans and heat through. Fill pockets with hot chili, sprinkle with cheese and serve.

POCKET WITH HASH FILLING (4 servings)

1 15-oz. can roast beef hash
1 cup diced tomato
½ cup diced green pepper
1 Tbsp. chili powder
¾ cup grated Cheddar cheese
2 cornmeal pitas, halved
Hot pepper sauce

Heat hash. Add tomatoes, green pepper, and chili powder. Mix well and heat through. Spoon hash filling into pockets and top with grated cheese. Serve immediately. Pass the hot sauce.

POCKET NACHO (6 servings)

1 small can refried beans
2 cups grated sharp Cheddar cheese
1 medium-sized ripe avocado
1 Tbsp. lemon juice
¼ tsp. garlic salt
2 tsp. grated onion
2 Tbsp. sour cream
Chili salsa
3 cornmeal pitas, halved

Heat beans in saucepan; spoon into pockets. Add cheese and heat in 350°F. oven until cheese melts.
Peel, seed, and mash avocado. Add lemon juice, salt, onion, and sour cream. Spoon over beans and cheese. Add salsa to taste and serve.

PORK AND APPLE PATTIES IN CORNMEAL (6 servings)

⅔ cup grated pared apple
1 lb. ground pork
½ cup soft bread crumbs
2 tsp. minced onion
1 egg yolk, beaten
½ tsp. monosodium glutamate
¼ tsp. mace
¼ tsp. nutmeg
⅛ tsp. salt
⅛ tsp. pepper
2 Tbsp. cooking oil
3 cornmeal pitas, halved
Applesauce, heated

Combine first 10 ingredients. Mix well and form into 6 patties. Cook in hot oil until well done. Place a pattie in each pocket and top with warmed applesauce.

SOUTH OF THE BORDER POCKETS (4 servings)

1 lb. ground beef
1 onion, chopped
¼ tsp. salt
¼ tsp. pepper
½ tsp. marjoram
¼ tsp. thyme
1 Tbsp. chili powder
2 Tbsp. chopped parsley
¼ cup tomato paste
¼ cup water
2 cornmeal pitas, halved

Brown beef and onion. Drain fat. Add remaining ingredients (except pita) and simmer together 15 minutes.
Fill pockets and serve with grated cheese, chopped chili peppers, diced olives, or chopped tomatoes, if desired.

TACO IN A POCKET (12 servings)

1 lb. ground beef
1 garlic clove, minced
1 onion, chopped
1 cup tomato sauce
1 Tbsp. Worcestershire sauce
1 tsp. chili powder
1 tsp. cumin
6 cornmeal pitas, halved
Shredded lettuce
Grated Cheddar cheese
Chopped Spanish onion
Chopped tomatoes
Chopped black olives
Taco sauce

Brown beef in skillet, breaking meat up with fork. Drain fat. Add garlic, onion, Worcestershire sauce, chili powder, and cumin. Mix well and simmer in skillet for 30 minutes.

Spoon beef mixture into pockets; top with lettuce, cheese, onion, tomatoes, black olives, and taco sauce.

TAMALE FILLING (8 servings)

¼ lb. pork sausage
1 lb. ground beef
1 cup finely chopped onion
½ cup finely chopped celery
½ cup finely chopped green pepper
2¼ cups tomato puree
1¼ cups whole kernel corn, drained
2 tsp. salt
2½ tsp. chili powder
½ tsp. cumin
¼ tsp. pepper
1 cup cold water
½ cup corn meal
1 cup sliced pitted black olives
¾ cup grated Cheddar cheese
4 cornmeal pitas, halved

Cook sausage, breaking up meat with fork; pour off fat. Add beef to skillet and cook until beef begins to brown. Add onion, celery, and green pepper. Cook until meat is well browned. Stir in tomatoe puree, corn, salt, chili powder, cumin, and pepper. Cover and bring mixture to a boil over high heat. Simmer 15 minutes.

Mix together cold water and corn meal; gradually add cornmeal mixture to simmering meat mixture, stirring constantly. Cook until mixture thickens. Stir in olives.

Turn into casserole and bake at 350°F., 1 hour. Cut into 8 squares and place a square into each pocket. Top with Cheddar cheese, stand upright in loaf pan and broil until cheese melts. Garnish with additional olives, if desired.

Chapter 3

Rye Pita and Fillings

RYE PITA

1½ cups lukewarm water
1½ Tbsp. active dry yeast
1 Tbsp. molasses
½ tsp. vegetable salt
2 cups whole wheat pastry flour
1 Tbsp. caraway seeds

   Combine lukewarm water, yeast, and molasses in mixing bowl and set aside in warm place until frothy. Stir in salt, flour, and caraway seeds; turn onto floured board and knead for approximately 10 minutes. Divide dough into 12 balls and roll each ball into a 6" round, 1/8" thick.
   Place rounds on lightly greased cookie sheets, cover with damp cloth and let rise in warm place for approximately 55 minutes.
   Bake in preheated 500°F. oven for 8 minutes.

AVOCADO SWISS FILLING (4 servings)

2 ripe avocados
2 Tbsp. lemon juice
2 cups grated Swiss cheese
2 cups alfalfa sprouts
2 Tbsp. yogurt or mayonnaise
Salt and pepper to taste
2 rye pitas, halved

Peel, pit, and slice avocado. Sprinkle with lemon juice, then toss with cheese and sprouts. Spread yogurt (or mayonnaise) on inside of pockets. Add filling and season with salt and pepper.

BAKED BRAUNSCHWEIGER FILLING (6 servings)

$1\frac{1}{2}$ lbs. Braunschweiger liver sausage, cut into 6 pieces
6 slices bacon
6 slices onion
6 slices tomato
6 mushrooms
3 Tbsp. prepared mustard
1 Tbsp. horseradish
3 rye pitas, halved

Wrap a slice of bacon around each piece of sausage, secure with a toothpick and place in a baking dish. Bake in preheated 350°F. oven 25 minutes. Combine mustard with horseradish. Spread mixture on insides of pockets.

Remove toothpicks from baked sausages and place a piece of bacon-wrapped sausage in each pocket. Add a slice of onion, tomato, and mushroom cap.

Top with additonal mustard, if desired.

BEEF-BACON SCRAMBLE IN A PITA (2 servings)

2 cups diced corned beef
2 slices bacon
1 onion, chopped
2 eggs, beaten
1 rye pita, halved

In small skillet, cook bacon until crisp; remove and drain. Cook onion and beef in bacon drippings until onion is golden brown. Add eggs and crumble bacon to pan, continue to cook until eggs are set. Season to taste. Fill pockets with beef-bacon mixture.

BEEF BURGUNDY FILLING (6 servings)

2 lbs. round steak, cut into thin strips
1/4 cup flour
1/4 cup margarine
1/2 cup chopped onion
1 Tbsp. finely chopped parsley
1 clove garlic, minced
1 bay leaf
1 6-oz. can mushrooms, drained
1 cup Burgundy
3 rye pitas, halved

Coat meat strips with flour. Brown meat in margarine in skillet, one half at a time. Add onions, parsley, garlic, and bay. Bring to boiling; reduce heat and simmer, covered, 30 minutes. Add mushrooms and Burgundy; simmer 30 minutes longer. Spoon into pockets.

BEEF STROGANOFF FILLING (8 servings)

*2 lbs. beef tenderloin,
   cut into ¼" thick strips*
¼ cup flour
1½ tsp. salt
¼ tsp. pepper
¼ cup butter
1 clove garlic, minced
1 cup chopped onion
1 lb. mushrooms, sliced
2 Tbsp. butter
3 Tbsp. flour
1 can undiluted beef broth
1 Tbsp. tomato paste
1 cup sour cream
4 rye pitas, halved
Paprika

Combine ¼ cup flour with salt and pepper. Melt ¼ cup butter in skillet. Coat meat with flour mixture and brown in butter in skillet. Add garlic, onion, and mushrooms; saute´ until onion is golden brown. Move meat and vegetables aside. Add 2 Tbsp. butter, and 3 Tbsp. flour; blend well. Add tomato paste and broth. Mix well with beef and vegetables. Cook until thickened. Add sour cream and heat through.

Spoon filling into pockets. Sprinkle with paprika.

CODFISH HASH IN RYE (6 servings)

2 cups flaked, salt codfish
3 Tbsp. melted margarine
1 onion, minced
1 clove garlic, minced
3 cups diced, boiled potatoes
½ cup water
¼ tsp. pepper
3 rye pitas, halved
Tomato sauce, warmed

In skillet, combine margarine, fish, onion, garlic, and potatoes. Stir in pepper and water. Cook slowly, stirring occasionally until potatoes are browned.
Fill pockets with hash. Top with warmed tomato sauce.

CORNED BEEF SUPREME (4 servings)

¼ cup mayonnaise
2 Tbsp. sour cream
1 Tbsp. horseradish
½ head lettuce, finely shredded
¼ tsp. salt
¼ tsp. pepper
2 4-oz. pkg. sliced corned beef
1 red apple, cored and diced
3 sweet pickles, chopped
2 rye pitas, halved

Combine all ingredients (except pita). Mix well. Chill. Fill pockets with mixture just prior to serving.

EGGS, COUNTRY STYLE (2 servings)

⅓ cup diced ham or cooked country-style sausage
⅓ cup grated cooked potato
2 Tbsp. butter or margarine
2 eggs, slightly beated
2 Tbsp. milk or cream
Salt and pepper to taste
¼ cup Monterey Jack cheese
1 rye pita, halved

Melt butter or margarine in skillet. Add meat and potato; cook until potatoes are lightly browned.
Mix together eggs, milk, salt and pepper. Pour over meat and potato mixture and scramble. Cook until eggs are set.
Fill pockets with mixture; place on a baking sheet and sprinkle with cheese. Broil in oven until cheese melts.

FALAFEL IN RYE POCKET (8 servings)

2 cans (20-oz. each) chick peas, drained
3 slices bread
3 bottled cherry peppers
3 sprigs parsley
3 eggs
½ tsp. garlic powder
¼ tsp. salt
¼ tsp. pepper
Peanut oil for frying
4 rye pockets, halved
1 cup tomato sauce
1 hot pepper, minced
Dash salt

Grind together chick peas, bread, peppers, and parsley. Add eggs, garlic powder, salt, and pepper. Let mixture stand 1 hour, then form into 3" balls; flatten slightly.
Heat oil in skillet to 375°F. Fry falafel in hot oil until golden; drain well on paper towels.
Place falafel in pockets and top with sauce.

HAM AND SWISS IN RYE (2 servings)

¼ lb. thinly sliced ham
1 cup grated Swiss cheese
1 to 2 Tbsp. mayonnaise
1 rye pita, halved

Spread mayonnaise on the insides of pockets. Stuff with ham. Sprinkle cheese on top of ham. Stand pockets upright in loaf pan and heat in 450°F. oven until cheese melts.

KNACKWURST-SWISS PITA MELT
(4 servings)

1 16-oz. pkg. knackwurst
2 rye pitas, halved
¼ cup margarine or butter, softened
1 8-oz. can sauerkraut, drained
½ cup shredded Swiss cheese
1 small tomato, thinly sliced
½ small green pepper, sliced into thin rings

Cut knackwurst in half lengthwise. Broil on rack in oven until lightly browned on both sides.
Spread insides of pockets with margarine. Place 2 knackwurst halves in each; add ½ cup of sauerkraut and ⅛ cup of cheese. Stand pockets upright in loaf pan and broil until cheese melts. Garnish each pocket with tomato and green pepper.

RED FLANNEL HASH IN RYE (6 servings)

1 1-lb. can julienne beets
2 1-lb. cans corned beef hash
2 Tbsp. minced onion
3 rye pitas, halved

Drain beets well. In large bowl, break up hash with fork; mix in beets and onions. Heat thoroughly in lightly greased skillet. Stuff pockets and serve at once.

REUBEN POCKET (4 servings)

½ lb. thinly sliced corned beef
1 cup drained sauerkraut
1 cup grated Swiss cheese
Thousand Island dressing
2 rye pitas, halved

Combine corned beef, sauerkraut and cheese in mixing bowl. Spread insides of pockets generously with dressing. Stuff with filling. Wrap each pocket in foil and heat in oven or on grill until cheese melts. Serve at once.

ROAST BEEF PITA BOY (6 servings)

½ cup olive oil
1 lb. cold roast beef, thinly sliced
2 green peppers, seeded, and sliced into rings
1 Spanish onion, thinly sliced
3 rye pitas, halved

Brush insides of pockets generously with olive oil and pile in beef, peppers, and onions.

RYE FILLED WITH LIVER AND ONIONS (6 servings)

1 lb. liver, cut into thin strips
½ tsp. salt
¼ tsp. pepper
2 Tbsp. bacon drippings
¼ cup margarine
1 lb. onions, thinly sliced
⅔ cup sliced mushrooms
¼ cup chopped green pepper
3 rye pitas, halved

Salt and pepper liver. Heat drippings and margarine in skillet. Sauté liver and onions in skillet until liver is done. Add mushrooms and green pepper. Heat through. Fill pockets with mixture.

SALMON-PINEAPPLE FILLING (4 servings)

8 oz. cream cheese, softened
2 Tbsp. milk
1 Tbsp. dill weed
1 7¾-oz. can salmon, drained
2 Tbsp. lemon juice
¼ tsp. salt
¼ tsp. pepper
1 8-oz. can crushed pineapple, drained
2 rye pitas, halved

Combine all ingredients, except pita. Mix well. Chill. Fill pockets with mixture just before serving.

SOYBEAN FILLING (4 servings)

1½ Tbsp. rice wine vinegar
1½ tsp. soy sauce
1½ tsp. sesame oil
½ tsp. honey
¼ tsp. dry mustard
¼ tsp. finely minced ginger root
1 tsp. toasted sesame seeds
1½ cups cooked soy beans
1 ripe tomato, diced
½ cup sliced mushrooms
¼ cup diced Cheddar cheese
¼ cup chopped green onion
½ cup pitted black olives, halved
2 rye pitas, halved

Combine vinegar, soy sauce, sesame oil, honey, mustard, ginger root, and sesame seeds. Marinate soybeans in mixture 1 hour.
Add tomato, mushrooms, cheese, and green onion. Toss well. Spoon mixture into pockets. Garnish with chopped olives.

SWEDISH MEATBALLS IN RYE (6 servings)

1 lb. ground beef
½ lb. pork sausage
1 Tbsp. minced onion
¼ cup bread crumbs
1 egg
½ tsp. salt
¼ tsp. pepper
Dash nutmeg
2 Tbsp. butter
4 tsp. flour
1 cup milk
3 rye pitas, halved

Combine meat, onion, bread crumbs, egg, salt, pepper, and nutmeg. Shape into balls; brown in butter. Remove meatballs from pan and add flour and milk to pan drippings, stirring to make gravy. Add meatballs and simmer gently 30 minutes, basting occasionally. Spoon filling into rye pockets. Serve immediately.

TUNA-CHUTNEY-CHEESE FILLING (4 servings)

2 8-oz. pkg. cream cheese, chilled
2 Tbsp. chopped mango chutney
½ tsp. curry powder
1 can mandarin oranges, drained
1 can tuna, drained and flaked
2 rye pitas, halved

Cut cheese into cubes and toss with chutney, curry, oranges, and tuna. Fill pita pockets with mixture, stand pockets upright in loaf pan, and broil in oven until cheese begins to melt.

Chapter 4

Sesame Pita and Filling

SESAME PITA

1½ cups lukewarm water
1 pkg. active dry yeast
2 tsp. honey
½ tsp. salt
3½ cups all-purpose flour
½ cup toasted sesame seeds

Add yeast and honey to lukewarm water. Set aside in warm place until mixture becomes frothy. Stir in salt, flour, and sesame seeds. Turn onto floured board and knead for 10 minutes. Divide dough into 12 balls and roll each ball into a 6" circle, ⅛" thick. Place on lightly greased cookie sheets, cover with damp cloth and allow to rise in warm place 45 minutes.

Bake in preheated 500°F. oven 5 to 7 minutes or until lightly browned.

CHICK-A-PITA (4 servings)

¼ cup flour
¼ tsp. seasoning salt
¼ tsp. pepper
1 egg
¾ cup dry bread crumbs
1 lb. boned and skinned chicken breasts
Oil for frying
1 cup mayonnaise
¼ cup bottled chili sauce
¼ cup sweet pickle relish
2 tsp. sugar
¼ tsp. dry mustard
¼ tsp. onion powder
2 sesame pitas, halved
1 tomato, sliced
1 cup shredded lettuce

Combine flour, salt, and pepper. Beat egg slightly. Heat oil, in frying pan, to 375°F. Cut chicken breasts into 4 sections. Coat each piece of chicken with flour mixture, dip the chicken into the beaten egg, then coat with bread crumbs. Fry chicken in hot oil, turning occasionally until golden brown (approximately 15 minutes). Drain on paper towels.

Mix together mayonnaise, chili sauce, relish, sugar, mustard, and onion powder. Spread mixture on inside of pita pockets.

Place a piece of fried chicken in each pocket and add tomato and lettuce.

CHICKEN LIVERS SUPREME (6 servings)

½ lb. chicken livers, in bite-sized pieces
2 Tbsp. butter or margarine
2 cups sliced fresh mushrooms
¼ cup chopped green onions
½ cup sour cream
1½ tsp. soy sauce
1½ tsp. chili sauce
Pepper to taste
3 sesame pitas, halved

In skillet, sauté livers in butter for approximately 10 minutes. Add mushrooms and onions; cook 5 minutes longer.
Combine sour cream, soy sauce, and pepper. Add to liver mixture and heat, stirring constantly. Fill pockets with mixture and serve at once.

CHILI LAMB FILLING (2 servings)

¼ lb. ground lamb
1 Tbsp. margarine
2 cups kidney beans, drained
½ cup chili sauce
½ cup chopped onion
1 sesame pita, halved

Brown lamb in margarine; drain fat. Add beans and chili sauce. Heat through. Spoon into pockets and sprinkle onions over filling.

CHINESE PORK FILLING (2 servings)

1/2 cup finely chopped uncooked pork
1 Tbsp. peanut oil
1 5-oz. can water chestnuts, drained and sliced
1 pkg. (7-oz.) frozen Chinese pea pods, thawed
1 tsp. monosodium glutamate
1 cup chicken broth
1 1/2 Tbsp. cornstarch
2 Tbsp. cold water
Soy sauce
1 sesame pita, halved

Brown pork in hot oil in skillet. Add next 4 ingredients. Steam, covered, over high heat 3 minutes. Combine cornstarch and 2 Tbsp. cold water. Add cornstarch mixture to broth and vegetable mixture. Cook and stir until thickened. Add soy sauce to taste and spoon into pockets. Serve at once.

CRAB CAKES IN POCKETS (4 servings)

1/4 cup butter
1 small onion, minced
2 Tbsp. green pepper, minced
1 pimiento, minced
3 Tbsp. flour
1/4 cup clam juice
1/4 cup cream
1 egg yolk
1 tsp. Worcestershire sauce
Dash hot pepper sauce
8 oz. crab meat
1 1/2 cups fresh bread crumbs
2 tsp. chopped parsley
2 sesame pitas, halved
Tartar or cocktail sauce

Heat 3 Tbsp. butter in skillet; saute' onion, green pepper, and pimiento. Add flour; cook and stir 2 minutes. Add clam juice and cream. Cook until thickened, stirring constantly.

Mix in yolk, Worcestershire sauce, hot pepper sauce, crab meat, ¾ cup of bread crumbs, and parsley. Chill for 2 or more hours, then shape into 4 cakes. Roll in remaining bread crumbs. Heat remaining 1 Tbsp. butter in skillet and brown on both sides. Reduce heat and cook for 6 to 8 minutes. Place a patty in each pocket and top with tartar or cocktail sauce.

GREEN BEANS AND PORK IN A POCKET (4 servings)

1½ cup pork, cut into 1" strips, ¼" thick
3 Tbsp. soy sauce
½ tsp. garlic powder
1 tsp. sesame seeds
1 medium onion, sliced
1 pkg. frozen French cut green beans,
*   thawed and drained*
1 Tbsp. bacon drippings
2 sesame pitas, halved

In skillet, cook pork in bacon drippings until pork is white. Add garlic powder, soy sauce, sesame seeds, and onion; cook and stir 10 minutes. Add green beans and cook 10 minutes longer.

Warm pitas in hot oven 30 seconds. Fill with bean-pork mixture.

HAWAIIAN LAMB FILLING (4 servings)

1 lb. boned lamb, cubed
1½ cups grated coconut
1½ cups milk
½ cup chopped onion
1 clove garlic, minced
2 Tbsp. butter
2 tsp. curry powder
½ tsp. salt
½ tsp. powdered ginger
1 Tbsp. flour
1 Tbsp. water
2 tsp. lemon juice
2 sesame pitas, halved

Soak coconut in milk for 1 hour. Saute´ onion and garlic in butter. Add curry, salt, and ginger. Blend flour and water; add to sauteed mixture. Cook a few minutes. Strain milk from coconut (reserve coconut) and add milk to mixture, along with meat, and simmer 1 hour. Add lemon juice and half of the reserved coconut. Spoon into pockets and serve at once.

LAMB AND MARINATED ONIONS IN SESAME (4 servings)

1 tsp. dried mint leaves
1 Tbsp. chopped parsley
½ tsp. thyme
¼ tsp. salt
Dash pepper
¼ cup vinegar
½ cup olive oil
2 sweet Spanish onions, sliced
4 cups diced cooked lamb
2 sesame pitas, halved

Combine mint, parsley, thyme, salt, pepper, vinegar, and oil.

Place onions in shallow dish; pour dressing over onions and allow to marinate overnight.

At serving time, remove onions from marinade and toss with lamb. Stuff lamb-onion mixture into pockets. Serve with remaining marinade, if desired.

ORIENTAL CHICKEN FILLING (8 servings)

5 cups cooked diced chicken breasts
1½ cups pineapple juice
¼ cup cornstarch
2 tsp. monosodium glutamate
5 Tbsp. soy sauce
1¼ cups brown sugar
⅔ cup vinegar
Dash garlic salt
4 sesame seed pitas, halved

Combine juice, cornstarch, monosodium glutamate, soy sauce, brown sugar, vinegar, and garlic salt in saucepan. Bring to simmer over medium heat, stirring constantly. Remove from heat after mixture thickens. Stir in chicken. Fill pockets with mixture and serve immediately.

OYSTER LOAF IN SESAME (6 servings)

6 slices white bread, crumbled
1½ cups chopped fresh oysters
3 eggs, beaten
½ cup evaporated milk
½ tsp. salt
Dash pepper
1 tsp. poultry seasoning
3 Tbsp. minced onion
1 green pepper, finely chopped
1 Tbsp. margarine
¼ cup each chopped celery and parsley
3 sesame pitas, halved
Chili sauce
Lemon wedges

Combine bread crumbs with oysters and mix thoroughly. Add eggs, milk, salt, pepper and poultry seasoning.
Melt margarine in skillet. Add onion and green papper; sauté. Add oyster mixture, celery, and parsley. Mix well, then turn mixture into greased loaf pan. Bake in 375°F. oven for 30 minutes. Turn onto platter to cool. Cut loaf into 6 slices.
Place a slice of oyster loaf into pocket; squeeze lemon wedge over filling and top with chili sauce.

PINEAPPLE CHICKEN SALAD PITA (2 servings)

1 cup cooked chicken, cubed
1 cup cubed pineapple, fresh or canned
¼ cup mayonnaise
½ cup diced celery
¼ cup chopped macadamia nuts or almonds
Salt to taste
1 sesame pita, halved

Combine chicken, pineapple, mayonnaise, celery, nuts, and salt. Chill. Fill pockets with mixture just before serving.

POCKET CRAB SALAD (2 servings)

1 cup crab meat
⅓ cup mayonnaise
½ cup chopped celery
1 Tbsp. minced green onion
2 Tbsp. minced sweet pickle
2 hard-cooked eggs, chopped
Salt and pepper to taste
1 sesame pita, halved
Paprika

Combine crab, mayonnaise, celery, onion, pickle, eggs, salt and pepper. Chill.
Fill pockets with filling and garnish with a dash of paprika.

POCKET OF EGG FOO YUNG (8 servings)

3 cups fresh mung bean sprouts
1 medium onion, chopped
6 eggs, beaten
½ green pepper, chopped
¼ lb. mushrooms, chopped
½ tsp. salt
¼ tsp. pepper
¼ cup margarine
4 sesame pitas, halved
Soy sauce

Combine sprouts, onion, eggs, green pepper, mushrooms, salt, and pepper in mixing bowl.
Melt margarine in skillet. Pour ⅔'s of a cup of egg mixture into skillet, forming a small omelet approximately 4" in diameter. Repeat with egg mixture, forming small omelets and leaving at least ½" between each. Cook until bottoms of omelets are browned; turn and brown other side. Keep cooked egg foo yung warm until all egg mixture has been cooked.
Place egg foo yung patties in pockets. Serve with soy sauce.

POCKET OF SOLE, POLYNESIAN STYLE (2 servings)

½ lb. fillet of sole
½ cup lime juice (fresh)
¼ cup olive oil
Lettuce leaves
1 sesame pita, halved

Marinate sole in lime juice at least 4 hours; then simmer in juice until fish is cooked. Chill.
Brush inside of pockets with olive oil. Line pockets with lettuce leaf and add chilled fish.

SESAME FULL OF CHOP SUEY (4 servings)

½ lb. lean beef, cut into strips
1 cup sliced onion
1 Tbsp. salad oil
1 cup beef broth
1 green pepper, cut into strips
½ cup diced celery
1 Tbsp. cornstarch
1 Tbsp. soy sauce
2 tsp. water
½ tsp. sugar
2 sesame pitas, halved

Brown meat and onion in oil. Add broth; cover pan and let simmer 15 minutes. Add celery and green pepper and simmer 10 minutes longer.
Combine cornstarch, soy sauce, sugar and water. Stir into meat mixture and cook until thickened. Spoon into pockets. Serve at once.

SESAME PITA CHEESE BURGER (2 servings)

4 thin hamburger patties
2 Tbsp. chopped onion
¼ cup shredded lettuce
2 slices American cheese
6 slices dill pickle
¼ cup mayonnaise
1 Tbsp. chili sauce
1 Tbsp. sweet pickle relish
½ tsp. sugar
1 sesame pita, halved

Fry hamburger patties.
Meanwhile, combine mayonnaise, chili sauce, relish, and sugar. Spread sauce on inside of pockets.
Sandwich cheese between two cooked hamburger patties and heat until cheese begins to melt. Slip meat-cheese patty into each pocket. Add lettuce, onion and pickle slices. Serve at once.

SWEET AND SOUR MEATBALL FILLING (6 servings)

½ lb. meat loaf mix
1 Tbsp. minced onion
1 Tbsp. soy sauce
1½ Tbsp. cornstarch
½ cup pineapple juice
½ cup pineapple tidbits
1 Tbsp. brown sugar
1½ Tbsp. vinegar
1 Tbsp. soy sauce
½ tsp. chicken bouillon
½ cup diced green pepper
3 sesame pitas, halved

Combine first 3 ingredients and shape into small balls. Bake in 350°F. oven 20 minutes. Drain. Mix cornstarch with remaining ingredients (except green peppers and pita) in saucepan and cook until thickened. Add meatballs and peppers. Spoon into pockets and serve at once.

TUNA PATTIES IN SESAME (4 servings)

1 7-oz. can tuna, drained
½ cup minced onion
½ tsp. seasoned salt
¼ tsp. pepper
2 Tbsp. diced celery
1 tsp. freshly chopped tarragon
   (or ½ tsp. dried)
1 egg, beaten
¼ cup cracker crumbs
¼ cup margarine
2 sesame pitas, halved
1 lemon, cut into wedges

Combine tuna, onion, salt, pepper, celery, tarragon, egg, and cracker crumbs. Mix well; form into 4 patties.
Melt margarine in skillet. Brown patties in margarine. Place a patty in each pocket and serve with lemon wedge.

Chapter 5

Sourdough Pita and Fillings

"Sourdough," the word itself carries a certain mystery. Its mere mention brings to mind visions of life on the frontier — the Klondike gold rush, a tiny homesteader's cabin on the vast Dakota prairie, chuck wagons and trail drives, the crusty old trapper leading a fur-laden pack string down from the mountains in spring. In Alaska, the title "Sourdough" is used with pride to differentiate those who have survived at least one winter in the Far North from the lowly "Chechaquo," or newcomer.

My first experience with sourdough cooking came while living in Anchorage as a young boy durng the early 50's. I can still recall the day my Father came home from work, grinning from eat to ear, and, with great pride, announced that a friend had just given him some 50 year old "starter." We quickly gathered around to see the wonderous brew, for, in those days, one did not bestow such a gift lightly. I could hardly contain my disappointment when he produced a jar of what appeared to be a thick, rancid pancake batter. All doubts were erased the next morning when I sat down to my first stack of sourdough pancakes — they were so light I had to keep them pinned to my plate with a fork!

Mystery and nostalgia aside, what is sourdough? Webster's defines it as "fermented batter of flour and water used to leaven fresh dough." While there are no accurate records of its first use, it is safe to assume sourdough has been around since shortly after man learned how to grind grain into flour. Sourdough cooking is an art that is as much at home in the modern kitchen of today as it was in the camps and on the trail a century ago.

The Tools

Only a modest investment is required to get started. You will need the following:

1 2-quart crock, wide mouthed glass jar, or plastic container with loose fitting lid.
1 large glass or plastic mixing bowl
1 wooden or plastic spoon
1 2-cup glass or plastic measuring cup

The Starter

With "tools" at hand, you are now ready to create your starter. Choose either of the recipes below, depending on your taste.

SOURDOUGH STARTER

1½ to 1¾ cup warm water
1 package active dry yeast
2 cups flour

WHOLE WHEAT SOURDOUGH STARTER

1¾ to 2 cups warm water
1 package active dry yeast
2 cups whole wheat flour

Combine the water and yeast in large mixing bowl, stir in flour to form a stiff batter. Set bowl in warm, draft-free spot and allow starter to work for 12 hours. Place starter in crock, cover and allow to set at room temperature for 24 hours. That's all there is to it!

The Rules

There are six basic rules for sourdough cooking. By following them exactly, you will insure your "starter" a long and productive life.

1. Add only flour and warm (not hot or cold) water to the starter — never sugar, salt, milk, oil, etc.
2. Do not allow the starter to come in contact with metal. Sourdough is acidic and contact with metal will taint its flavor.
3. Do not place the starter in a tightly sealed container. The gases produced by fermentation could cause the container to break — a very messy situation.
4. Refrigerate the starter when it will not be used for a prolonged period — a week or more. Refrigeration causes the starter to go dormant, thereby avoiding over-fermentation.
5. Bring the starter to room temperature before using. This is automatically accomplished by setting the sponge as described below.
6. Allow the starter to work at room temperature for an extra 24 hours after it has been used before refrigerating.

Setting The "Sponge"

Your starter is a "yeast factory" and, as such, requires a supply of raw materials (flour and water) and the right environment (room temperature) to produce. These ingredients are provided when you set the sponge.

About twelve hours before you plan to bake, determine the quantity of batter (or sponge) required. The following, when added to your starter, will provide two cups of usable batter:

1½ to 2 cups warm water
2 cups of white or whole wheat flour

At this point, a few words of warning are in order. If your starter has been dormant for sometime, a layer of vile looking liquid will have formed on top. It will be brownish in color when white flour is used and gray/greenish in the case of whole wheat. Don't be alarmed — the starter hasn't spoiled! The liquid is just the natural result of fermentation and should be stirred back into the dough.

Several years ago, I gave a close friend, who, now in the interest of domestic and professional tranquility, I will allow to remain anonymous, some of my highly prized fifteen year old starter. A couple of months later, I checked with her to see how "they" were getting along. Quite apologetically, she told me that, despite following my instructions to the letter, the starter had "died." She then proceeded to describe the above mentioned liquid. At the time I didn't have the heart to tell her she had unceremoniously flushed a perfectly healthy starter down the drain.

To set the sponge proceed as follows: Remove the starter from the crock and place in large bowl; add warm water and mix thoroughly. Stir in flour to form a thick batter. Place the bowl in a warm, draft free place and allow to work for twelve hours. Clean the crock thoroughly. I prefer to set my sponge the evening before and allow it to work overnight. It is hard to beat the special aroma which greets you the next morning. Your starter can convert up to eight cups of flour into usable batter overnight, so you may wish to allow some extra batter for a batch of pancakes or waffles. Just be certain your mixing bowl is large enough for the sponge (which will double in bulk during this process).

After the sponge has set, gently stir in any crust which has formed and return two cups of batter to the crock. This then becomes your starter. Allow the crock to remain at room temperature for 24 hours, then refrigerate. The batter that remains is now ready for use wherever sourdough starter or batter is called for.

SOURDOUGH PITA

1 cup lukewarm water
1 pkg. active dry yeast
3 tsp. sugar
1 cup sourdough starter
¾ tsp. salt
½ tsp. baking soda
2½ cups all-purpose flour
½ cup all-purpose flour

WHOLE WHEAT PITA

1 cup lukewarm water
1 pkg. active dry yeast
1 Tbsp. honey
1 cup whole wheat sourdough starter
½ tsp. sea salt
½ tsp. baking soda
2¾ cup pastry whole wheat flour
½ cup pastry whole wheat flour

Combine yeast and sugar in lukewarm water and allow to stand until frothy.

Stir in starter, salt, and soda. Add 2½ cups all-purpose flour. Put ½ cup flour on board. Add dough and knead 10 minutes. Divide dough into 12 balls. Roll each into a 6" circle, ⅛" thick, and place on lightly greased cookie sheets. Cover with damp cloth and let rise in warm place for 45 minutes.

Bake in preheated 500°F. oven 4 to 5 minutes or until lightly browned.

ALASKAN POCKET BREAKFAST (2 servings)

½ cup smoked salmon, broken into small pieces
1 Tbsp. butter or margarine
2 large eggs
¼ tsp. salt
Black pepper to taste
2 Tbsp. butter or margarine
⅓ cup grated medium Cheddar cheese
1 sourdough pita, halved

Melt 1 Tbsp. butter in small skillet; add salmon and heat.
In large skillet, melt 2 Tbsp. butter. Add eggs, salt, and pepper to skillet and scramble. Add salmon before eggs have set.
Fill pockets with cooked egg-salmon mixture. Arrange pockets on a cookie sheet, top with cheese, and broil in oven until cheese melts.

ARTICHOKE-CRAB FILLING (2 servings)

4 marinated artichoke hearts, diced
1 medium tomato, diced
½ lb. fresh crab meat
2 hard-cooked eggs, riced
3 Tbsp. Thousand Island dressing
1 sourdough pita, halved

Combine artichokes, tomato, crab, eggs, and dressing.
Spread pockets with mayonnaise or dressing, if desired. Fill pockets with crab mixture.

CREAMED CHICKEN AND HAM FILLING (4 servings)

¼ cup margarine
½ cup chopped onion
¼ cup flour
2 tsp. prepared mustard
Dash salt and pepper
1 cup milk
1 cup chicken broth
¼ lb. mushrooms, sliced
1 cup cooked diced chicken
1 cup diced cooked ham
2 sourdough pitas, halved
Paprika

Melt margarine in saucepan; add onion and cook until tender. Blend in flour, mustard, salt, and pepper. Add milk and chicken broth. Bring to boiling and cook 2 minutes, stirring constantly. Stir in mushrooms, chicken, and ham. Heat.

Spoon into sourdough pockets. Sprinkle with paprika and serve at once.

CURRIED SEAFOOD IN SOURDOUGH (6 servings)

½ lb. scallops
½ lb. cooked shrimp, deveined
¼ lb. crab meat
3 Tbsp. butter
3 Tbsp. flour
2 Tbsp. curry powder
1 cup cream
½ cup chicken broth
3 sourdough pitas, halved

Boil scallops in chicken broth for 5 minutes. Melt butter in skillet; add flour and blend; stir in curry. Add cream, stirring until smooth. Stir in broth, scallops, shrimp, and crab. Heat thoroughly over low heat. Spoon mixture into pockets and serve at once.

FLAMING TURKEY POCKETS (4 servings)

6 cups diced cooked turkey
2 Tbsp. butter
1 cup canned Bing cherries with juice
6 Tbsp. red wine
½ tsp. basil
½ tsp. thyme
½ tsp. marjoram
2 Tbsp. cornstarch
2 Tbsp. brandy
2 sourdough pitas, halved

Sauté turkey in butter; set aside. Simmer cherries with ⅔ cup cherry juice, wine, basil, thyme and marjoram for fifteen minutes. Mix cornstarch with small amount of water; stir into cherry mixture. Cook until thickened. Stir in turkey. Fill pockets with cherry-turkey filling. Stand pockets upright in glass loaf pan. Pour ½ Tbsp. brandy into center of filling of each pocket. Ignite and serve.

FLYING SAUCERS (6 servings)

4 tsp. red wine vinegar
1 tsp. olive oil
¼ tsp. salt
¼ tsp. coarse pepper
¼ tsp. oregano
6 sourdough pitas
1 8-oz. pkg. sliced bologna
1 8-oz. pkg. sliced Swiss cheese
1 cup shredded lettuce
1 8-oz. pkg. sliced salami
¼ cup sliced red cherry peppers
½ cucumber, thinly sliced
1 small tomato, thinly sliced
1 small red onion, thinly sliced
5 pitted ripe olives, sliced

Combine vinegar, oil, salt, pepper, and oregano; set aside. Make a slit along the length of the top side of pitas. Brush inside of pitas with vinegar-oil mixture.

Fill pitas, through slit, with remaining ingredients. Add more dressing, if desired. Garnish with whole black olives on toothpicks.

HAM PATTIES WITH CHERRY SAUCE (4 servings)

3 cups ground cooked ham
½ cup dry bread crumbs
2 eggs, beaten
¼ cup milk
¼ tsp. pepper
¼ cup margarine
1 cup cherry preserves
2½ Tbsp. lemon juice
¾ tsp. cinnamon
¼ tsp. ground cloves
2 sourdough pitas, halved

Combine ham, crumbs, eggs, milk, and pepper. Shape into four patties.

Melt margarine in skillet. Brown patties in margarine. In saucepan, combine cherry preserves, lemon juice, cinnamon, and cloves. Heat to boiling.

Place ham patties in pockets and spoon sauce over filling.

LAMB KABOBS IN SOURDOUGH (8 servings)

1 cup rosé wine
½ cup orange juice
⅔ cup finely chopped onion
⅓ cup chili sauce
¼ cup salad oil
1 clove garlic, minced
1 Tbsp. brown sugar
½ tsp. salt
1 tsp. crushed oregano
¼ tsp. pepper
2 lbs. boneless lamb, cubed
12 whole mushrooms
2 green peppers, cut in 1½" squares
4 sourdough pitas, halved

Combine first 10 ingredients in large mixing bowl. Add lamb cubes; cover bowl and marinate 3 hours at room temperature. Thread lamb, peppers, and mushrooms alternately on skewers and grill over charcoal 15 to 25 minutes, basting frequently with marinade. Serve kabobs in sourdough pockets. Sprinkle with additional marinade, if desired.

LASAGNA IN SOURDOUGH (6 servings)

¾ lb. Italian sausage
½ cup chopped onion
¼ cup chopped celery
¼ cup grated carrot
1 7½-oz. can tomatoes, cut-up
1 6-oz. can tomato paste
½ cup water
¼ tsp. salt
1½ tsp. dried oregano
1½ cups ricotta cheese
¼ cup grated Parmesan cheese
2 Tbsp. snipped parsley

3 cups grated mozzarella cheese
3 sourdough pitas, halved

Cook sausage, onion, celery, and carrot in skillet until browned. Drain off fat. Stir in tomatoes, tomato paste, water, salt, and oregano. Simmer, covered, 15 to 20 minutes, stirring occasionally. Combine ricotta, Parmesan, and parsley.
Spoon meat sauce into pita pockets, top with a spoonful of ricotta mixture, then sprinkle with cheese. Repeat layering, then place stuffed pockets upright in a loaf pan and bake 350°F. 15 to 20 minutes.

MEATBALLS ITALIANO IN POCKETS
(4 servings)

1 egg, slightly beaten
1½ Tbsp. milk
¼ cup dry bread crumbs
¼ tsp. salt
½ lb. hamburger
¼ lb. bulk sausage
½ cup chopped onion
¼ cup chopped green pepper
½ cup tomato sauce
1 can (6-oz.) tomato paste
¼ cup Burgundy
½ tsp. sugar
1 tsp. garlic powder
½ tsp. oregano
¼ tsp. rosemary
2 sourdough pitas, halved

Combine egg, milk, crumbs, salt, beef, and sausage. Mix well. Form into 1½" balls. Brown in skillet along with onion and green pepper. Drain fat. Stir in remaining ingredients. Cover and simmer 15 minutes, stirring occasionally. Spoon into pockets. Sprinkle with Parmesan cheese, if desired. Serve at once.

PAPA JOE'S PITA (4 servings)

½ lb. lean ground beef
6 green onions, sliced
1 Tbsp. butter
4 eggs, beaten
Salt and pepper to taste
2 cups sliced fresh mushrooms
½ 10-oz. pkg. chopped spinach,
   cooked and drained
2 sourdough pitas, warmed and halved

Sauté beef and onions in butter until meat is browned. Squeeze spinach to remove excess moisture. Add to meat, along with mushrooms, pour eggs over and scramble. Season to taste. When eggs are cooked, fill pockets with mixture and serve at once.

PICKLED HERRING IN SOURDOUGH (4 servings)

2 jars pickled herring, drained
1 medium Bermuda onion, thinly sliced
2 sourdough pitas, halved

Cut herring into bite-sized pieces. Toss with onion slices, then stuff into pockets.

PITA WITH ITALIAN SAUSAGE (4 servings)

1 large green pepper, seeds removed
2 medium onions
1½ lbs. Italian sausage
1 Tbsp. oregano
Bottled Italian-style tomato sauce, heated
2 sourdough pitas, halved

Cut green peppers into thin strips. Thinly slice onions, separating into rings. Sauté peppers and onions in oil over medium heat. Add sausages to skillet, prick with fork and brown slowly, turning frequently. Add oregano to skillet, cover, and cook over low heat 12 to 15 minutes. Stuff pita pockets with sausage mixture and top with Italian-style sauce.

POCKET FISHWICH (4 servings)

1 lb. fish fillets
Milk
¾ cup flour
1 tsp. sugar
1 tsp. baking powder
¼ tsp. salt
¾ cup beer
Flour
Oil for deep frying
2 sourdough pitas, halved
Tartar sauce

Rinse fillets and cut into triangular shapes; soak in milk for 1 hour.
Sift together ¾ cup flour, sugar, baking powder, and salt. Stir in beer.
Drain fillets well; dip in flour, then dip in batter. Deep fry in hot (375°F.) oil for 4 minutes each side. Drain well on paper towels.
Spread inside of pockets with tartar sauce. Add fish fillets and serve with additional tartar sauce or lemon wedges.

POLYNESIAN BEEF FILLING (6 servings)

1½ lbs. beef round steak, sliced diagonally
1 Tbsp. cornstarch
¼ tsp. salt
¼ tsp. garlic salt
¼ tsp. celery seed
¼ cup salad oil
1½ cups sliced celery
1 medium onion, sliced
3 Tbsp. cooking sherry
3 Tbsp. soy sauce
1 20-oz. can pineapple chunks
1 6-oz. pkg. pea pods
10 cherry tomatoes, halved
3 sourdough pitas, halved

Combine cornstarch, salts, and celery seed. Sprinkle over meat. Brown beef strips quickly in hot oil; add remaining ingredients and heat through. Fill pockets at once.

SIRLOIN-MUSHROOM FILLING (6 servings)

1 lb. beef sirloin, cut into thin strips
1 Tbsp. salad oil
¼ cup soy sauce
¼ cup sugar
½ Tbsp. cooking sherry
½ cup consomme'
1 onion, sliced
½ lb. mushrooms, sliced
½ cup sliced celery
1 small can bamboo shoots, sliced
½ cup sliced green onions
3 sourdough pitas, halved

Brown meat in oil. Combine soy sauce, sugar, wine, and consomme'. Add half to pan with beef. Add vegetables and simmer 3 minutes. Add remaining sauce and simmer 3 minutes longer. Remove vegetables and beef with slotted spoon and stuff into pockets. Add a spoonful of pan drippings and serve immediately.

SMOKED WHITEFISH AND CREAM CHEESE (2 servings)

1 3-oz. pkg. cream cheese,
   at room temperature
1/4 lb. smoked whitefish
   (or kippered salmon)
1 1/4"-slice of large mild Bermuda
   onion, cut in half
1 sourdough pita, halved

Heat pockets for a few minutes. Spread inside of pockets with cream cheese. Place a half slice of onion in each pocket and add fish. Goes great with sliced tomatoes and cold beer.

SOUR CREAM PITA BURGERS (6 servings)

2 lbs. ground beef
1 cup dairy sour cream
2 Tbsp. Worcestershire sauce
2 Tbsp. minced onion
1/2 tsp. salt
1 cup cornflakes
3 sourdough pitas, halved

Combine beef, sour cream, Worcestershire sauce, onion, cornflakes, and salt. Form meat into 6 patties. Broil 4 inches from heat for 4 minutes; turn and cook to desired doneness. Fill pockets with patties and top with chopped onions, B-B-Q sauce, catsup, hot mustard, or other desired toppings.

SWEET AND SOUR PORK FILLING (4 servings)

1 1/2 lbs. lean pork shoulder,
   cut into 1/2" cubes
3 Tbsp. cooking oil
1 1/2 cups chicken bouillon

¼ cup chopped onion
1 cup pineapple chunks
3 small tomatoes, chopped
¼ cup cornstarch
½ cup sugar
½ cup vinegar
1 Tbsp. soy sauce
¾ cup pineapple juice
2 sourdough pitas, halved

Brown pork in oil; add bouillon. Cover and cook over low heat 20 minutes. Add onion and pineapple; cook 10 minutes longer. Add tomatoes.
Blend cornstarch with sugar, vinegar, soy sauce, and pineapple juice. Add to pork mixture. Cook and stir until mixture thickens. Spoon into pockets and serve at once.

WESTERN-STYLE EGGS IN PITA (2 servings)

⅓ cup diced ham
1 green onion, chopped
2 Tbsp. diced green pepper
¼ cup chopped tomato
¼ cup diced mushrooms
3 Tbsp. butter
2 large eggs
2 Tbsp. milk or cream
Pepper to taste
⅓ cup grated medium Cheddar cheese
1 sourdough pita, halved
2 thin slices of tomatoes

In skillet, melt 1½ Tbsp. butter and saute' ham and vegetables lightly. Remove from heat.
Melt remaining butter in skillet. Scramble eggs together with milk, salt, and pepper and cook in butter in skillet. Mix in vegetables and ham mixture and as much of the pan drippings as desired.
Fill pockets with egg-vegetable mixture and place pockets on cookie sheet. Arrange a slice of tomato on each half and top with grated cheese. Place pockets under broiler and broil until cheese melts.

Chapter 6

Triticale Pita and Fillings

TRITICALE PITA

1½ cups lukewarm water
1 pkg. active dry yeast
2 tsp. honey
½ tsp. vegetable salt
2¼ cups triticale flour
1 cup whole wheat pastry flour

    Add yeast and honey to lukewarm water and stir to dissolve yeast. Set aside in warm place until frothy. Add salt and flours, stirring well. Turn dough onto lightly floured board and knead 10 minutes. Divide dough into 12 balls and roll each into a 6" circle, ⅛" thick. Place rounds on greased cookie sheets, cover with damp cloth, and allow to rest in warm place for 45 minutes.
    Bake in preheated 500°F. oven for 5 to 6 minutes.

ARTICHOKE-TUNA FILLING (4 servings)

3 Tbsp. olive oil
1 Tbsp. lemon juice
1 7-oz. can tuna, drained and flaked
6 cooked artichoke hearts, quartered
1 large tomato, chopped
¼ Spanish onion, sliced into rings
2 tsp. minced fresh dill
Salt and pepper to taste
2 Triticale pitas, halved

Combine all ingredients (except pita), mix well. Chill for several hours. Fill pockets with mixture just before serving.

BEEF STRIPS, BELGIUM STYLE (4 servings)

1 lb. steak, cut into thin strips
1 onion, chopped
1 Tbsp. vinegar
¼ tsp. sugar
¼ tsp. marjoram
¼ tsp. thyme
¼ tsp. rosemary
1 cup beer
3 Tbsp. margarine
2 triticale pitas, halved

Combine beef and onions with vinegar, sugar, herbs, and beer. Marinate for 4 to 6 hours. Remove meat and onion from marinade and sauté in margarine for a few minutes. Fill pockets and serve at once.

BEEF ZINGER (4 servings)

1 lb. beef sirloin, cut into thin strips
½ tsp. powdered ginger
½ tsp. chili powder
½ tsp. garlic powder
2 Tbsp. grated lemon rind
3 Tbsp. margarine
½ tsp. sugar
1 Tbsp. plum jam
1½ Tbsp. lemon juice
½ tsp. salt
2 triticale pitas, halved

Combine ginger, chili powder, garlic powder, and lemon rind. Coat meat with mixture and brown in margarine.
Combine sugar, plum jam, lemon juice, salt, and ½ cup water. Add to meat and simmer until meat has cooked to desired doneness. Using slotted spoon, fill pockets with mixture and serve at once.

BROCHETTS (8 servings)

2 lbs. top round steak, cut into 1" cubes
1 cup vegetable oil
¼ cup vinegar
2 tsp. salt
1 tsp. pepper
1 tsp. paprika
2 cloves garlic, minced
1 Tbsp. oregano
Dash hot pepper sauce
4 triticale pitas, halved

Combine all ingredients except pita and marinate meat in refrigerator 4 to 12 hours.
Skewer beef and grill or charcoal to desired doneness, basting with marinade. Serve in pita pockets.

CLAM FRITTERS IN TRITICALE (6 servings)

4 cups minced clams
4 beaten egg yolks
4 egg whites, beaten stiff
2 cups dried bread crumbs
1 tsp. salt
1 tsp. pepper
2 Tbsp. chopped parsley
2 Tbsp. chopped chives
2/3 cup milk
1/4 cup vegetable oil
3 triticale pitas, halved
1 lemon, cut into wedges
Cocktail sauce

Combine clams, yolks, crumbs, salt, pepper, parsley, and chives in mixing bowl. Add milk. Fold in egg whites. Heat oil in frying pan. Drop batter into pan, forming patties. Cook, turning once, until each side is browned. Place a fritter in each pocket. Serve with lemon wedge and cocktail sauce.

CLUB IN A PITA (6 servings)

3 Tbsp. Thousand Island dressing
3 triticale pitas, halved
1 8-oz. pkg. sliced Swiss cheese
1 6-oz. pkg. sliced cooked turkey
1 8-oz. pkg. sliced cooked ham
3 cups alfalfa sprouts
6 ripe olives

Spread dressing on inside of pockets. Fill pockets with cheese, turkey, and ham. Stand upright in loaf pan and heat pockets under broiler until cheese melts. Remove pockets from heat and top with sprouts. Garnish with an olive.

DILLED VEAL FILLING (6 servings)

1 lb. ground veal
4 slices bacon, cooked crisp and crumbled
¼ cup dry bread crumbs
¼ cup milk
1 beaten egg
¼ tsp. dillweed
1 chicken bouillon cube
1½ cups boiling water
½ tsp. Worcestershire sauce
1 Tbsp. cornstarch
3 triticale pitas, halved

Combine veal, bacon, crumbs, milk, egg, and dill. Mix thoroughly. Shape into small balls.

Dissolve bouillon in boiling water; add Worcestershire sauce. Pour into skillet. Add meatballs and bring to boiling. Cook, covered, 15 minutes. Turn meatballs once during cooking. Blend 1 Tbsp. cold water into cornstarch; stir into meatball-sauce mixture. Cook and stir over low heat until mixture thickens. Spoon into pockets and serve at once.

GARLIC LAMB KABOBS IN A POCKET (6 servings)

1½ lb. boneless lamb,
  cut into 1" cubes
1 cup garlic salad dressing
2 medium green peppers,
  cut into squares
1 16-oz. can small onions
6 skewers
3 triticale pitas, halved

Marinate meat in dressing 2 hours at room temperature; turn occasionally. Drain meat. Brush inside of pockets with marinade. Skewer lamb, peppers, and onions and broil 4" from heat source for 15 minutes or until desired doneness. Serve in pockets.

GERMAN POTATO SALAD FILLING
(6 servings)

6 medium potatoes
Water
2 Tbsp. salad oil
1 medium onion, sliced
¼ cup thinly sliced celery
1 16-oz. pkg. knackwurst, sliced diagonally
⅓ cup white wine vinegar
1 chicken bouillon cube
1 Tbsp. sugar
½ tsp. salt
½ tsp. dry mustard
¼ cup chopped parsley
3 triticale pitas, halved

Cook potatoes in water until fork tender; drain and cool. Peel potatoes and cut into bite-sized pieces.

In skillet, sauté onion and celery in oil. Remove vegetables and brown knackwurst in skillet. Stir in potatoes, onion mixture, vinegar, bouillon, sugar, salt, mustard, and ⅔ cup water. Cook until potatoes are heated and mixture thickens. Gently stir in parsley. Spoon into pockets and garnish with parsley sprig.

LATIVA FILLING (8 servings)

1 lb. cold roast veal, diced
3 medium potatoes, boiled peeled, and diced
2 dill pickles, minced
½ cup cooked beets, minced
½ onion, chopped
3 hard-cooked eggs, chopped
1 3-oz. can herring fillets, cut up
½ small jar pickled cocktail mushrooms, cut in half
1 cup sour cream
½ cup mayonnaise
4 triticale pitas, halved

Combine all ingredients (except pita) and chill. At serving time, fill pockets with mixture. Serve at once.

MARINATED ONION AND LAMB FILLING (2 servings)

½ tsp. dried mint leaves
½ Tbsp. chopped parsley
¼ tsp. thyme
¼ tsp. salt
Dash pepper
2 Tbsp. vinegar
¼ cup olive oil
1 large sweet Spanish onion, sliced
2 thick slices cooked lamb
1 triticale pita, halved

Combine mint, parsley, thyme, salt, pepper, vinegar, and oil. Place onions in shallow dish; pour dressing over and allow onions to marinate overnight.
Spread inside of pockets with marinade. Add onions and lamb. Serve at once.

MINTED LAMB PATTIES IN POCKETS (4 servings)

1½ lb. ground lamb
3 Tbsp. chopped parsley
1 egg, beaten
½ tsp. salt
½ tsp. monosodium glutamate
¼ tsp. allspice
¼ cup mint jelly
2 triticale pitas, halved
Sour cream

Combine lamb, parsley, egg, and seasonings. Mix lightly. Form mixture into 4 patties. Broil patties 3" from heat source for approximately 9 minutes on each side. Brush patties with jelly and broil a minute or two longer. Place a patty in each pocket and top with sour cream.

SAUSAGE-APPLE FILLING (6 servings)

18 sausage links
2 Tbsp. water
4 medium apples, cut into ½" thick rings
⅓ cup firmly packed brown sugar
½ tsp. nutmeg
½ tsp. cinnamon
3 triticale pitas, halved

Remove seeds from center of apples.
Place sausage in skillet with water. Cover and cook 10 minutes. Pour off liquid and brown links over medium heat. Remove sausage to warm platter. Add apples to skillet and cook in drippings over low heat 8 minutes. Sprinkle apples with sugar, nutmeg, and cinnamon. Cook gently until sugar is melted.
   Place sausages in each pocket. Add apple slices and serve at once.

SCALLOPS-PINEAPPLE KABOBS (6 servings)

1 lb. scallops
¼ cup butter, melted
1 tsp. salt
½ tsp. each paprika and pepper
10 slices lean bacon
1½ cups drained pineapple chunks
3 triticale pitas, halved
Lemon wedges

   Season butter with salt, paprika, and pepper. Dip scallops in butter.
   Fry bacon gently for 4 to 5 minutes. Drain well. Cut bacon into thirds crosswise. Alternate scallops, bacon, and pineapple on 6 skewers. Place skewers across a baking dish and bake in hot 450°F. oven for 20 minutes, turning once. Serve in pockets with lemon wedges.

TABULI IN A POCKET (4 servings)

1 cup bulgar wheat
Boiling water
1 cup peeled and chopped tomato
½ cup chopped parsley
½ cup chopped mint leaves
½ cup chopped onion
½ cup olive oil
¼ cup lemon juice
½ tsp. salt
Dash pepper
2 triticale pitas, halved

Place wheat in oven-proof bowl and pour over boiling water to cover. Let stand 2 to 2½ hours; drain well. Add tomato, parsley, mint and onion. Combine remaining ingredients in jar with tight fitting lid; shake well to mix. Pour dressing over wheat mixture and toss lightly. Chill overnight to blend flavors.

Just prior to serving, spoon tabuli into pockets; garnish with fresh mint sprig, if desired.

WEST INDIES STEAK FILLING (4 servings)

1 lb. steak, cut in thin strips
2 cloves garlic, minced
½ tsp. thyme
½ tsp. mace
½ tsp. nutmeg
1 tsp. salt
½ tsp. pepper
2 Tbsp. minced parsley
3 onions, sliced
¼ cup vinegar
2 Tbsp. olive oil
2 triticale pitas, halved

Marinate steak in a combination of all other ingredients (except pita) for 4 to 12 hours.

Remove meat and onions from marinade and sauté in butter or margarine to desired doneness. Brush insides of pockets with leftover marinade. Fill with steak and onions. Serve at once.

Chapter 7

Whole Wheat Pita and Fillings

WHOLE WHEAT PITA

1½ cups lukewarm water
1 pkg. active dry yeast
2 tsp. honey
½ tsp. sea salt
3 cups whole wheat flour

 Put water, yeast, and honey in large bowl and let stand in warm place until frothy. Stir in salt and flour, then knead dough for about 10 minutes on floured board. Divide dough into 12 balls and roll each into a 6" round, ⅛" thick.
 Place rounds on lightly greased cookie sheets, cover with damp cloth, and let rise in warm place for about 45 minutes.
 Preheat oven to 500°F. Bake bread for 5 to 8 minutes, or until lightly browned.

HONEY-CRACKED WHEAT PITA

1½ cups lukewarm water
1½ Tbsp. active dry yeast
2 Tbsp. honey
½ tsp. vegetable salt
3 cups whole wheat pastry flour
½ cup cracked wheat

Combine lukewarm water, yeast, and honey in mixing bowl and set aside in warm place unti frothy. Stir in salt, flour, and cracked wheat. Turn onto floured board and knead dough for approximately 10 minutes. Divide dough into 12 balls and roll each into a 6" round, ⅛" thick.

Place rounds on lightly greased cookie sheets, cover with damp cloth, and let rise in warm place for approximately 55 minutes.

Bake in preheated 500°F. oven for 6 to 8 minutes.

ARTICHOKE VINAIGRETTE IN PITA

(2 servings)

1 Tbsp. Dijon mustard
1 Tbsp. minced shallots
3 Tbsp. wine vinegar
½ cup olive oil
2 cups cooked, drained artichoke hearts
½ cup chopped watercress
1 whole wheat pita, halved

Combine mustard, shallots, vinegar, and oil. Mix well. Pour over artichoke hearts, cover and marinate 24 hours.

Brush insides of pockets with marinade. Add drained artichokes and watercress. Great served with mild cheese and a light wine.

BEEF BURMA IN WHOLE WHEAT
(4 servings)

1 lb. steak, thinly sliced
2 onions, sliced
1 tsp. turmeric
½ tsp. chili powder
1 tsp. powdered ginger
3 Tbsp. sesame oil
Salt to taste
2 whole wheat pitas, halved

Toss meat strips with onions, turmeric, chili powder, and ginger. Sauté in hot oil to desired doneness. Season with salt. Fill pockets and serve immediately.

BURGER ORIENTAL FILLING (6 servings)

1 lb. ground beef
1 cup sliced celery
1 cup chopped onions
¼ tsp. garlic powder
1 cup water
1 pkg. brown gravy mix
¼ cup soy sauce
½ tsp. brown sugar
¼ tsp. pepper
2 cups mung bean sprouts
1 cup mushrooms, sliced
3 whole wheat pitas, halved

Sauté beef, celery, onions, with garlic powder in lightly oiled skillet, until meat is no longer pink. Stir in water, gravy, soy sauce, sugar, and pepper. Cook, stirring, until thickened. Add sprouts and mushrooms. Heat thoroughly. Spoon into pockets and serve at once. Toasted sesame seeds make an attractive garnish when sprinkled over filling.

EAST INDIAN LAMB FILLING (4 servings)

2½ cups cooked, diced lamb
½ cup shredded coconut
½ cup thinly sliced celery
1 can mandarin oranges, drained
½ cup mayonnaise
½ cup yogurt
2 Tbsp. wine vinegar
2 tsp. curry powder
¼ tsp. pepper
2 whole wheat pitas, halved

In bowl, combine lamb, coconut, celery, and oranges. Mix together remaining ingredients (except pita). Pour mixture over lamb filling and toss well. Fill pockets and serve at once.

GREEK GYROS (6 servings)

½ lb. ground lamb
½ lb. ground beef
1 cup fresh bread crumbs
1 clove garlic, minced
2 Tbsp. chopped parsley
1 tsp. chili powder
½ tsp. cumin
Dash cayenne
1 small onion, chopped
½ cup sour cream
½ tsp. dill weed
¼ tsp. salt
2 tsp. lemon juice
1 tomato, thinly sliced
3 cups shredded lettuce
3 whole wheat pitas, halved

Mix together lamb, beef, bread crumbs, garlic, parsley, chili, cumin, and cayenne in mixing bowl. Mix well and form into a 1"-thick patty 4" wide by 6" long. Broil patty, turning once until well browned on each side (approximately 15 minutes). Let cool for 15 minutes before slicing.

Mix together onion, sour cream, dill, salt, and lemon juice. Stir well. Slice meat into thin strips. Fill each pocket with meat, lettuce, tomatoes, and sour cream-onion mixture. Stand pockets upright in loaf pan and heat in 375°F. oven for about 5 minutes. Serve at once.

HOT GINGER STEAK FILLING (4 servings)

1 lb. steak, cut into thin strips
3 gingersnaps
¼ cup vinegar
1 onion, sliced
¼ tsp. freshly ground pepper
½ cup water
¼ tsp. basil
½ tsp. sugar
2 whole wheat pitas, halved

Soak gingersnaps in vinegar 10 to 15 minutes. Combine with meat and remaining ingredients (except pita) and simmer gently until meat has reached desired doneness. Fill pockets with mixture and serve at once.

ITALIAN CUBE STEAKS IN PITA (6 servings)

6 cube steaks
2 Tbsp. margarine
6 slices Mozarella cheese
¾ cup water
1 8-oz. can tomato sauce
2 cloves garlic, minced
1 tsp. dried oregano leaves
½ tsp. dried basil, crushed
¼ tsp. dried rosemary
3 whole wheat pitas, halved

In skillet, brown steaks in margarine for a few minutes. Turn and brown other side. Top with cheese. Remove to platter and keep warm.
Add water, tomato sauce, garlic, oregano, basil, and rosemary to skillet. Heat thoroughly.
Place cheese-topped meat in pockets; top with sauce. Serve at once.

ITALIAN EGGPLANT FILLING (6 servings)

Olive oil
1 medium green pepper, thinly sliced
¼ cup flour
½ tsp. salt
1 small eggplant, cut into ¼" thick slices
1 15-oz. can tomato sauce
2 Tbsp. sugar
1 tsp. oregano leaves
3 whole wheat pitas, halved
1 8-oz. pkg. Mozarella cheese,
    cut into thin strips

Sauté green pepper in oil until tender. Remove from oil and keep warm. Coat eggplant slices with flour and salt. Cook in hot oil in skillet a few at a time. Drain well. Keep warm.
Mix together tomato sauce, sugar, and oregano. Fill pockets with

warm eggplant slices and green pepper. Top with sauce. Add cheese; stand pockets upright in loaf pan and broil until cheese melts.

MEAT 'N POTATOES IN POCKETS (4 servings)

2½ cups mashed potatoes
2 cups cubed cooked roast beef
2 hard-cooked eggs, chopped
½ cup pickle relish
1 Tbsp. chopped pimento
2 Tbsp. vinegar
2 Tbsp. mayonnaise
2 whole wheat pitas, halved

Combine all ingredients (except pita) and chill. Fill pockets with mixture just before serving.

POCKET FRANKS AND BEANS (6 servings)

6 frankfurters
¼ cup chopped onion
1 Tbsp. butter
3 cups beans with pork in tomato sauce
¼ cup catsup
2 tsp. brown sugar
3 whole wheat pitas, halved

Slice frankfurters lengthwise almost through. Brown franks and onions in butter in skillet. Add beans, catsup, and brown sugar. Cook slowly for 15 minutes. Serve in pockets.

POLISH PEASANT POCKETS (8 servings)

2 cups diced cooked pork
1 lb. sauerkraut, drained
½ cup sliced mushrooms
2 strips bacon, cooked and crumbled
2 tsp. chopped parsley
1 onion, chopped
2 kielbasa, sliced
1 cup red wine
½ tsp. sugar
4 whole wheat pitas, halved

Combine all ingredients (except pita) and bring to boiling over medium heat. Simmer gently 10 minutes. Drain excess liquid and fill pockets with kielbasa-sauerkraut mixture.

RUMAKI IN PITA (4 servings)

1 Tbsp. sugar
1 bay leaf
1 cinnamon stick
1 cup chicken stock
1 1"-piece ginger root
2 Tbsp. anise seed
1 crushed garlic clove
2 cups soy sauce
1 lb. chicken livers
1 can water chestnuts
½ lb. sliced bacon
Cooking oil
2 whole wheat pitas, halved
Soy sauce or hot Chinese mustard

Combine sugar, seasonings, stock, and soy sauce in saucepan. Bring to boiling, reduce heat and simmer 5 minutes. Add livers, bring to boil. Reduce heat and simmer 10 minutes. Remove livers from liquid. Cool. Cut water chestnuts in thirds. Wrap a piece of bacon around liver and section of water chestnut; secure with toothpick.

Fry bundles in hot oil until bacon is crisp. Drain well on paper towels. Remove toothpicks and fill pockets with bacon wrapped livers. Serve with soy sauce or hot mustard.

THE RED BARON (4 servings)

1 lb. cubed steaks, cut into julienne strips
1/4 cup soy sauce
3 Tbsp. brown sugar
2 Tbsp. lemon juice
1/4 tsp. ground ginger
1/4 tsp. pepper
2 Tbsp. salad oil
1 small head red cabbage, shredded
2 whole wheat pitas, halved

In medium-sized bowl, mix together soy sauce, brown sugar, lemon juice, ginger, and pepper. Add beef strips, stirring to coat well. Cover and refrigerate at least 3 hours, stirring occasionally.

In skillet, cook meat in oil until browned. Set aside. Add cabbage and remaining marinade to skillet and stir-fry until cabbage is tender-crisp. Add meat to cabbage, heat quickly, then spoon into pockets.

SHISH KABOBS IN PITA (8 servings)

1/2 cup Teriyaki sauce
1 lb. boneless steak, cubed
1 green papper, cubed
1/4 lb. small whole mushrooms
1 carton cherry tomatoes
1 small zucchini, diced
1/2 cup pitted black olives
1 small onion, eighthed
4 whole wheat pitas, halved
Teriyaki sauce

Marinate meat in Teriyaki sauce 3 hours. Skewer meat and vegetables on kabob skewers and grill over hot coals to desired doneness.

Fill pockets with grilled ingredients and serve with additional Teriyaki sauce.

STEAMED CLAMS IN A POCKET (6 servings)

6 dozen Little Neck or hard shell clams
Salted water to cover
1 cup water
¼ cup melted butter
1 Tbsp. lemon juice
3 whole wheat pitas, halved
Cocktail or tartar sauce

Soak clams in salted water to cover 3 to 4 hours. Drain; rinse well. Scrub clams and rinse again. Place clams on rack in pot with 1 cup water and steam 5 to 7 minutes. Cool slightly; remove clams from shells. Combine lemon juice with butter and toss with clams. Heat seasoned clams, then fill pockets and serve immediately. Pass the cocktail or tartar sauce.

TUNA-SPROUT POCKET SALAD (4 servings)

1 can (9½-oz.) tuna, drained
3 cups fresh spinach, torn
2 cups fresh mung bean sprouts
1 can water chestnuts, drained and sliced
2 Tbsp. sliced green onion
½ cup Russian dressing
2 whole wheat pitas, halved

Combine tuna, spinach, sprouts, chestnuts, and onion. Toss with dressing. Chill.
Fill pockets with tuna mixture.

TURKISH LAMB FILLING (4 servings)

6 lamb chops, cut into thin strips
½ cup wine vinegar
2 Tbsp. olive oil
½ onion, sliced
1 Tbsp. chopped parsley
2 whole cloves
2 peppercorns, crushed
2 whole wheat pitas, halved

Marinate lamb strips in mixture of vinegar, olive oil, onion, parsley, cloves, and peppercorns 3 hours. Remove meat and onion from marinade and stir-fry in hot skillet 5 minutes. Fill pockets and serve at once.

VEAL-OYSTER LOAF FILLING (6 servings)

½ pint oysters, drained and finely chopped
1 lb. ground veal
1¼ cups corn flake crumbs
½ cup minced onion
¾ cup evaporated milk
1 egg, beaten
½ tsp. salt
½ tsp. paprika
¼ tsp. marjoram
¼ tsp. thyme
3 whole wheat pitas, halved
Yogurt or sour cream

Combine oysters, veal, crumbs, onion, milk, egg, and seasonings. Pack lightly into loaf pan and bake 350°F. for 1½ hours. Unmold onto platter. Cool. Chill. Cut into 6 slices and place one in each pocket. Top filling with yogurt or sour cream.

Chapter 8

Hors d'oeuvre Pita Fillings

Hors d'oeuvre pita is made by following the instructions for any of the previous pita breads, then dividing dough into 30 balls, rather than 12. Roll dough into small circles; place circles on lightly greased cookie sheets; cover with damp cloth; and allow to rise in a warm place for 35 to 40 minutes. Bake in preheated 500°F. oven for 4 to 6 minutes, or until lightly browned. (Freeze for later use.)

AVOCADO-SALMON FILLING

1 ripe avocado
1 7¾-oz. can salmon
1 Tbsp. lemon juice
1 Tbsp. finely minced garlic
2 Tbsp. grated onion
¼ tsp. salt
4 dashes hot pepper sauce

Combine all ingredients in large bowl. Let stand at room temperature 1 hour.
Fill small pita pockets with mixture.

BEER-CHEESE FILLING

Great stuffed in rye pockets for a snack during N.F.L. half-time. A partially empty can of beer is bound to be lying around somewhere.

> ¾ cup beer
> ¾ lb. sharp Cheddar cheese, grated
> ⅛ lb. Blue cheese, crumbled
> ½ tsp. mustard
> 1 Tbsp. butter
> ½ tsp. Worcestershire sauce
> 1 dash hot pepper sauce
> 2 tsp. chopped chives

In blender container, blend beer and cheddar until smooth. Add remaining ingredients, except chives, and blend until smooth. Fill pockets and garnish with chives (if you want to get fancy).

BLACK OLIVE PATÉ FILLING

> 2 cups pitted black olives
> ¼ cup butter
> 1 medium onion, grated
> 1 tsp. black pepper

Put all ingredients in blender container and blend until smooth. Fill small pockets with a teaspoonful of mixture.

CLAM AND CHEESE FILLING

> 1 pkg. (3-oz.) softened cream cheese
> 1 can (7-oz.) minced clams, drained
> 1 tsp. soy sauce
> 1½ tsp. prepared mustard
> 1 Tbsp. minced onion

Mix ingredients well. Fill small pita pockets and chill until served.

CHEESE-CURRY FILLING

Best in basic or sourdough pita.

½ lb. sharp Cheddar cheese, grated
2 Tbsp. chutney, finely chopped
2 tsp. curry powder

Mix ingredients thoroughly and fill tiny pockets with mixture.

CHEESE SUPREME FILLING

½ cup dry cooking sherry
1 oz. softened butter
2 oz. sharp Cheddar cheese, grated
3 oz. cream cheese, softened
4 oz. Blue cheese, crumbled
5 oz. Gorgonzola cheese, grated
1½ Tbsp. Worcestershire sauce

Place all ingredients in large bowl and cream together with the back of a spoon. Place creamed mixture in smaller container and chill.
Stuff tiny pita pockets just before serving.

CHILI CON QUESTA

Keep the filling warm in a chafing dish and a tray of small cornmeal pita pockets at hand so that guests can serve themselves.

1 large onion, minced
2 small garlic cloves, minced
¼ cup butter
1 1-lb. 13-oz. can tomatoes
1 4-oz. can green chilies, seeded and minced
2 Tbsp. flour
1 cup evaporated milk
½ tsp. salt

4 drops hot pepper sauce
½ lb. Jack cheese, grated

Sauté onion and garlic in 2 Tbsp. butter. Add tomatoes and simmer until sauce becomes thick. Stir in chilies.

Make a white sauce with remaining butter, flour, and evaporated milk. Cook until thickened, then add to tomato mixture. Add salt and hot pepper sauce. Approximately 3 to 4 minutes before serving, add cheese and stir until melted.

CRABMEAT FILLING

2 7-oz. cans drained crabmeat
2 tsp. horseradish
2 Tbsp. lemon juice
2 Tbsp. minced green onions
½ tsp. salt
¼ tsp. pepper

Combine all ingredients. Chill. Fill small pockets just prior to serving and garnish with paprika.

DEVILED HAM FILLING

1 can (4½-oz.) deviled ham
2 Tbsp. mayonnaise
1 Tbsp. chopped sweet pickle
1 Tbsp. chopped pimento
2 tsp. chopped celery

Combine all ingredients and mix well. Fill small pockets with mixture, then chill.

FISHY ONION FILLING

¾ cup salad oil
1 egg yolk
1 Tbsp. grated lemon rind
¼ cup mashed capers
¼ cup lemon juice
6 anchovy fillets, minced
1 Tbsp. grated onion
1½ cups drained tuna, flaked

Blend ¼ cup oil, egg yolk, and 2 Tbsp. lemon juice together in small mixing bowl. Add remaining oil gradually.
Combine capers, lemon rind, anchovy fillets, tuna, and remaining lemon juice. Beat into egg-oil mixture. Chill.
Serve mixture inside tiny pockets.

GUACAMOLE

Guacamole filled Hors d' oeuvre-sized cornmeal pockets make an excellent beginning to a Mexican-style dinner.

2 large ripe avocados, peeled and mashed
1 medium tomato, peeled and chopped
2 cans mild green chiles, chopped
1 Tbsp. freshly squeezed lemon juice
Salt and pepper to taste

Combine all ingredients and mix well.

HERRING IN SOUR CREAM FILLING

1 16-oz. jar herring fillets, finely minced
1 cup sour cream
Juice of 1 lemon
1 large onion, diced
½ tsp. freshly ground pepper
1 tsp. salt

1 tsp. monosodium glutamate

Combine all ingredients and mix well. Chill at least 2 hours. Serve in bowl along side a tray of small pita pockets and let guests serve themselves.

LIVER FILLING

1 cup ground cooked liver
1 hard-cooked egg, riced
3 Tbsp. minced celery
2 Tbsp. minced onion
1 tsp. prepared mustard
¼ tsp. salt
¼ tsp. monosodium glutamate
¼ cup catsup

Combine all ingredients. Chill. Fill small pita pockets with mixture just before serving.

MUSHROOM FILLING

1 Tbsp. butter
¾ cup thinly sliced mushrooms
3 Tbsp. minced celery
3 Tbsp. chopped green pepper
2 Tbsp. chopped green onion
2 Tbsp. chopped parsley
1 Tbsp. lemon juice
3 Tbsp. mayonnaise
Salt and pepper to taste

Sauté mushrooms and celery in butter. Combine with remaining ingredients. Chill.
Fill tiny pockets and serve at once.

NEW ZEALAND FILLING (serves 6)

3 cups minced ham
1 cup chutney
1 cup chili sauce
1½ cup shredded Cheddar cheese

Combine all ingredients. Fill small pockets with mixture. Just before serving, heat hors d'oeuvres under broiler until cheese melts.

OLIVE-EGG FILLING

3 Tbsp. yogurt
1 Tbsp. lemon juice
2 hard-cooked eggs, riced
¼ cup minced black olives
1 clove garlic, minced
1 Tbsp. chopped parsley
1 Tbsp. snipped chives
¼ tsp. salt
¼ tsp. pepper
¼ tsp. paprika

Combine all ingredients and mix well. Chill mixture before filling small pita pockets.

SALMON FILLING

¼ cup mayonnaise
1 tsp. lemon juice
1 can (7¾-oz.) salmon, drained
¼ cup diced black olives
2 Tbsp. minced celery
¼ tsp. prepared horseradish

Combine all ingredients and mix well. Chill mixture before filling small pockets.

SEAFOOD FILLING

1 cup lobster
½ cup crabmeat
½ cup salmon (cooked)
¼ cup mayonnaise
¼ cup whipping cream

Combine all ingredients and mix well. Fill small pita pockets with mixture.

SMOKED FISH FILLING

¾ lb. smoked whitefish
1 8-oz. pkg. cream cheese, softened
3 Tbsp. cream
2 Tbsp. lemon juice
¼ tsp. liquid smoke
¼ tsp. garlic salt
1 small onion, thinly sliced

Skin and bone fish; flake. Combine remaining ingredients, except onion, and mix well. Cover; chill.

Stuff mixture into small pockets and serve with a slice of onion.

TURKISH EGGPLANT FILLING (serves 4 to 6)

This traditional Turkish hors d'oeuvre is excellent served in small whole wheat pita pockets.

2 small eggplants
1 medium onion, minced
1 1/2 tsp. salt
1/2 tsp. black pepper
2 Tbsp. olive oil
1 Tbsp. chopped parsley
1/4 cup lemon juice

Remove stems from eggplant and grill, whole, under moderate flame until skin begins to split.

Peel and mash eggplant. Add onion, salt, and pepper; beat smooth. Add oil. Fill small pockets with mixture and sprinkle with parsley and lemon juice.

Chapter 9

Dessert Pita and Filling

DESSERT PITA

1½ cups lukewarm water
1 pkg. active dry yeast
¼ cup sugar
¼ cup melted butter
3½ cups all-purpose flour
1 tsp. vanilla extract

Put water, yeast, and sugar in large bowl and let stand in warm place until frothy. Stir in cooled melted butter, flour, and vanilla. Turn dough onto floured board and knead 10 to 15 minutes. Divide dough into 14 balls and roll each into a 6" round, ⅛" thick.

Place rounds on cookie sheets and set in warm place for 45 minutes to rise.

Bake in preheated 500°F. oven for 5 to 7 minutes or until lightly browned.

APPLE-MINCE FILLING (6 servings)

1½ cups pared, chopped apple
3½ cups prepared mincemeat
1 Tbsp. lemon juice
1 tsp. grated lemon rind
3 dessert pitas, halved

Combine ingredients and mix thoroughly. Heat. Fill pockets with hot filling.

CARAMEL FLAN IN A POCKET (6 servings)

¾ cup sugar
1 Tbsp. water
3 eggs, beaten
1 can evaporated milk
1 tsp. vanilla
3 dessert pitas, halved

Combine ¼ cup sugar and 1 Tbsp. water in saucepan. Cook slowly, stirring constantly, until sugar caramelizes. Pour into flan pan.
In bowl, combine eggs, remaining sugar, milk, and vanilla. Beat well, then pour over caramelized sugar in pan. Set flan pan in baking pan filled with 1" water. Bake 350°F. 1 hour. Remove from heat and allow to cool in pan 15 minutes. Chill 3 hours, then invert onto platter. Cut into 6 wedges and place a wedge in each pocket. Spoon caramel sauce over flan. Also good topped with crushed sweetened berries.

CHERRY FILLING (6 servings)

6 cups pitted tart red cherries
1¾ cups sugar
½ cup quick-cooking tapioca
1 tsp. grated lemon rind
Dash salt
3 sweet pitas, halved

Place cherries in large bowl, sprinkle with sugar, tapioca, lemon rind, and salt. Mix lightly and set aside 10 minutes.

Pour cherry mixture into saucepan and bring to boiling, stirring constantly. Reduce heat and simmer gently 15 minutes. Add a little water, if necessary. Fill pitas while filling is hot; or chill filling for a warm weather dessert. Top with a dab of whipped cream, if desired.

COCONUT CHIFFON FILLING (6 servings)

¼ cup cold water
1 envelope unflavored gelatin
4 eggs, separated
1 cup milk
½ cup sugar
Dash salt
1 cup shredded coconut
1½ tsp. vanilla extract
¼ cup sugar
3 dessert pitas, halved

Sprinkle gelatin evenly over cold water. Let stand 5 minutes.

In top of double boiler, mix together slightly beaten egg yolks, milk, ½ cup sugar, and salt. Cook over simmering water, stirring constantly, until mixture coats spoon. Remove pan from simmering water and stir in softened gelatin. Blend in coconut and vanilla. Chill until mixture begins to gel, stirring occasionally.

Beat egg whites until frothy. Gradually add sugar and beat until whites form rounded peaks. Fold into chilled coconut mixture. Chill until firm.

Spoon into dessert pockets just before serving.

CREAMY BANANA FILLING (6 servings)

3 egg yolks
¼ cup sugar
1½ tsp. lemon juice
½ tsp. vanilla flavoring
1 8-oz. pkg. cream cheese, softened
3 Tbsp. milk
3 bananas, sliced
3 dessert pitas, halved

Beat together yolks, sugar, juice, and vanilla until thick. Gradually beat in cream cheese until mixture is smooth and fluffy. Beat in milk. Chill. At serving time, stir in sliced bananas. Spoon filling into pockets.

EASY LEMON FILLING (6 servings)

1 small can frozen lemonade concentrate
1 can sweetened condensed milk
1 small (4½-oz.) container imitation whipped topping
3 dessert pitas, halved

Combine lemonade and milk. Fold in whipped topping. Spoon into a bowl and refrigerate at least 2 hours.
Fill pockets with chilled filling just before serving.

FRESH APRICOT FILLING (6 servings)

1 Tbsp. lemon juice
4 cups sliced ripe apricots
¾ cup light brown sugar
¼ cup sugar
2 Tbsp. quick-cooking tapioca
¼ tsp. salt
2 Tbsp. butter, melted
3 dessert pitas, halved

Combine lemon juice with apricots, sugars, tapioca, salt, and butter. Mix well. Spoon into baking dish and bake at 350° F. 30 minutes. Fill pockets with warm filling.

FRESH PLUM FILLING (6 servings)

2 lbs. ripe plums, pitted and chopped
¾ cup light corn syrup
2 Tbsp. cornstarch
½ tsp. ground cinnamon
½ cup chopped walnuts
3 dessert pitas, halved

Combine plums, syrup, cornstarch, cinnamon, and walnuts in large saucepan. Heat to boiling; reduce heat and simmer 10 minutes. Cool slightly before filling pockets.

LEMON-CHEESE FILLING (8 servings)

1 lb. cream cheese
¾ cup sugar
1 Tbsp. flour
1 tsp. grated lemon rind
½ tsp. vanilla extract
2 eggs, slightly beaten
1 egg yolk
2 Tbsp. heavy cream
4 dessert pitas, halved

    Combine cheese, sugar, flour, rind, and vanilla. Beat until smooth. Add eggs, yolk, and cream. Blend well. Pour into round cake pan and bake 250°F. 45 minutes. Turn off heat. Let stand in oven 1 hour longer. Cool completely. Chill. Spoon into pockets just before serving.

MOCHA CHOCOLATE CREAM FILLING (4 servings)

½ cup cocoa powder
⅔ cup sugar
¼ cup flour
1 cup double strength coffee
1 cup cold milk
Dash salt
3 egg yolks, slightly beaten
2 Tbsp. melted butter
2 tsp. vanilla extract
2 dessert pitas, halved

    Combine cocoa with sugar, flour, and salt. Blend with 1 cup cold milk.
    Heat coffee in top of double boiler. Stir in cocoa mixture. Bring mixture to boiling, stirring constantly. Cook 3 minutes over medium heat. Then place saucepan over simmering water. Cover and cook 7 minutes.

Stir 3 Tbsp. of hot cocoa-milk mixture into egg yolks, then immediately blend into mixture in top of double boiler. Cook over simmering water 7 minutes, stirring frequently. Remove from heat. Stir in butter and vanilla. Cover; cool; then chill at least 2 hours.

Fill pockets just before serving.

PEACH CREAM FILLING (4 servings)

2 large peaches, peeled and sliced
½ cup whipping cream
1 small pkg. instant vanilla pudding and pie filling mix
¾ cup milk
½ tsp. lemon extract
2 dessert pitas, halved

Whip cream until stiff peaks form. Prepare pudding mix according to package directions, using only ¾ cup milk. Fold in whipped cream, lemon extract, and peaches. Chill at least 15 minutes before filling pockets.

PEAR CRUMBLE FILLING (6 servings)

2 Tbsp. sugar
1½ Tbsp. cornstarch
Dash nutmeg
1 1-lb. 13-oz. can pears, drained
1 cup pear liquid
1 tsp. grated lemon rind
2 tsp. lemon juice
2 Tbsp. butter
½ cup brown sugar, packed
½ cup chopped walnuts
½ tsp. cinnamon
3 dessert pitas, halved

Combine sugar, cornstarch, and nutmeg in saucepan. Slowly add pear liquid. Cook over medium heat, stirring until mixture thickens. Add rind and lemon juice. Stir well before adding butter and pear pieces. Spoon into baking dish.

Combine brown sugar, walnuts, and cinnamon in bowl. Sprinkle over pear mixture. Bake at 425°F. for 20 to 25 minutes. Cool slightly before filling pockets.

PECAN FILLING (8 servings)

3 eggs
¼ tsp. salt
½ cup brown sugar
1 cup light corn syrup
1 tsp. vanilla
2 Tbsp. melted butter
3 cups broken pecans
4 dessert pitas, halved

Beat eggs lightly; add salt and brown sugar; beat well. Add syrup, vanilla, and butter; beat well. Add pecans and pour into glass casserole and bake in preheated 350°F. oven 35 minutes. Remove from heat and stir well. Allow to cool 30 minutes before filling pockets. Can be served either warm or chilled.

PINEAPPLE CREAM FILLING (4 servings)

1 cup crushed pineapple, drained
1½ cups milk
½ cup sugar
2 Tbsp. cornstarch
Dash salt
½ cup cold milk
3 eggs, well beaten
1 tsp. vanilla extract
2 dessert pitas, halved

Scald 1½ cups milk in top of double boiler. Combine sugar, cornstarch, salt, and ½ cup cold milk. Gradually stir into scalded milk. Bring to boiling over direct heat, stirring constantly, for 3 minutes. Pour mixture in top of double boiler and place over simmering water. Cover and cook 12 to 15 minutes, stirring occasionally.

Mix eggs with 3 Tbsp. hot milk mixture; immediately blend into mixture in double boiler. Cook over simmering water 7 minutes, stirring. Cover and cool.

Stir in pineapple and vanilla. Chill several hours before filling pockets.

POCKET STRAWBERRY SHORT CAKE (4 servings)

1 quart fresh strawberries
¼ cup sugar
1 pint whipping cream
½ cup sugar
1 tsp. vanilla
2 dessert pitas, halved

Hull berries and mix with ¼ cup sugar. Set aside. Whip cream with ½ cup sugar until peaks form. Stir in vanilla.

Fill pockets with berries and top berries with whipped cream.

PUMPKIN CUSTARD FILLING (4 servings)

1 cup milk
1 cup canned pumpkin
½ cup sugar
1 tsp. cinnamon
½ tsp. nutmeg
½ tsp. vanilla
2 eggs, well beaten
Dash salt
2 dessert pitas, halved
Whipped cream

Pour milk into eggs and beat together. Add pumpkin, sugar, cinnamon, nutmeg, vanilla, and salt. Pour into custard pan and place in larger pan of water. Put pans in preheated 350°F. oven and bake 30 minutes. Chill.
Just before serving, fill pockets with chilled mixture and top with whipped cream.

RHUBARB FILLING (4 servings)

1 lb. rhubarb, cut into 1" pieces
1 cup sugar
1 tsp. grated lemon rind
½ tsp. cinnamon
1 Tbsp. lemon juice
2 Tbsp. butter
2 dessert pitas, halved

Combine rhubarb with sugar, lemon rind, cinnamon, and lemon juice. Spoon into 1½ qt. casserole and dot with butter. Bake at 350°F. 45 minutes. Cool to warm; spool warm filling into pockets.

SPICED APPLE FILLING (8 servings)

1 cup sugar
¼ cup flour
1 tsp. pumpkin pie spice
¼ tsp. salt
3 lbs. apples, pared, cored and sliced
2 Tbsp. melted butter
2 Tbsp. lemon juice
4 dessert pitas, halved

Combine all ingredients (except pita) and spoon into baking dish. Bake in preheated 400°F. oven 35 to 40 minutes.
Use as warm or chilled filling to fill pockets.

STRAWBERRY CHIFFON FILLING
(6 servings)

1 pkg. (3-oz.) strawberry flavored gelatin
⅔ cup boiling water
2 cups ice cubes
1 container (8-oz.) non-dairy whipped topping
2 cups fresh strawberries, sliced
3 dessert pitas, halved

Dissolve gelatin in boiling water. Add ice cubes and stir until gelatin is thickened. Remove any unmelted ice. Blend in non-dairy whipped topping; blend until smooth. Fold in fruit. Chill mixture 2 hours. Spoon filling into pockets; garnish with a whole fresh strawberry, if desired, and serve at once.

STRAWBERRY-RHUBARB FILLING
(6 servings)

¾ cup sugar
⅓ cup instant tapioca
¼ tsp. salt
2½ cups rhubarb, sliced
2 cups water
1½ cups strawberries, sliced
3 dessert pitas, halved

In saucepan, stir together sugar, tapioca, and salt. Stir in rhubarb and water. Cook and stir over medium heat until rhubarb is tender and mixture has thickened. Remove from heat and stir in strawberries. Chill. Spoon into pockets and serve at once.

QUICK APPLE-CHEESE FILLING (4 servings)

1 can (21-oz.) apple pie filling
¼ cup tiny cubes sharp Cheddar cheese
½ cup chopped pecans
¼ cup sugar, mixed with 2 tsp. cinnamon
2 dessert pitas, halved

Combine apple filling with cheese and pecans. Fill pockets and sprinkle filling with sugar-cinnamon mixture. Stand pockets upright in loaf pan and heat in 400°F. oven until cheese begins to melt.

Chapter 10

More Cold Fillings

BEAN SALAD FILLING (4 servings)

4 hard-cooked eggs, diced
2 cups kidney beans, drained
1/3 cup minced sweet pickles
1/2 cup finely chopped onion
3 Tbsp. sweet pickle liquid
1/2 cup mayonnaise
2 pitas, halved

Combine eggs, beans, pickles, and onion. Mix together pickle liquid and mayonnaise. Toss with egg-bean mixture. Chill. Serve in pita pockets.

CHINESE CHICKEN SALAD FILLING (4 servings)

2 cups diced, cooked chicken
1 cup drained pineapple tidbits
1 1/2 cups fresh mung bean sprouts
1 can (5-oz.) water chestnuts, sliced
2 Tbsp. sliced green onion
1/2 cup sour cream
1/2 tsp. ground ginger
2 pitas, halved

Combine ingredients (except pita), chill, then stuff into pockets.

COLD LAMB FILLING (2 servings)

1 cup cooked, diced lamb
¼ cup shredded coconut
½ cup thinly sliced celery
1 medium orange, peeled and sectioned
½ cup mayonnaise
2 Tbsp. wine vinegar
½ tsp. salt
1 tsp. curry powder
¼ tsp. pepper
1 pita, halved

Combine lamb, coconut, celery, and orange. Mix together mayonnaise, vinegar, salt, curry, and pepper; pour over lamb mixture and toss well.
Spoon mixture into pockets.

EGGPLANT SALAD FILLING (8 servings)

1 small eggplant,
  cut into julienne strips
3 small zucchini,
  cut into julienne strips
¼ cup olive oil
1 clove garlic, minced
1 small onion, diced
¼ lb. mushrooms, sliced
1 12-oz. bottle chili sauce
1 cup water
⅓ cup red wine vinegar
1 tsp. oregano leaves
1 tsp. sugar
½ tsp. fennel seeds
½ tsp. dry mustard
6 hard-cooked eggs
4 pitas, halved

In skillet, cook garlic, onion, and mushrooms in olive oil until

tender. Stir in chili sauce, water, vinegar, oregano, sugar, fennel, and mustard. Add eggplant to chili sauce mixture; heat to boiling. Reduce heat to low; cover and simmer 5 minutes. Add zucchini; cover and simmer 5 minutes longer, stirring occasionally. Chill.
Just before serving, dice eggs and gently stir into chilled eggplant mixture. Fill pockets. Garnish with toasted sesame seeds, if desired.

FAR EAST FILLING (4 servings)

2½ cups fresh mung bean sprouts
2½ cups cooked small shrimp, deveined
3 hard-cooked eggs, chopped
½ cup blanched almonds, slivered
¼ cup oil
2 Tbsp. vinegar
½ clove garlic, crushed
¼ tsp. ginger
½ tsp. soy sauce
2 pitas, halved

Combine sprouts, shrimp, eggs, and almonds. Mix together oil, vinegar, garlic, ginger, and soy sauce. Toss with shrimp mixture. Fill pockets with filling.

FRUITED CHICKEN FILLING (6 servings)

3 cups cubed cooked chicken
1 cup diced celery
1 11-oz. can mandarin oranges, drained
1 small can pineapple tidbits, drained
½ cup slivered almonds
½ cup mayonnaise
¼ tsp. salt
¼ tsp. marjoram
3 pitas, halved

Combine first eight ingredients. Chill. Mound into pita pockets just before serving.

GARBANZO AND MUSHROOM FILLING (2 servings)

1 cup chopped fresh mushrooms
¾ cup cooked garbanzo beans, mashed slightly
¼ cup minced celery
¼ cup minced sweet red pepper
2 Tbsp. minced onion
2 Tbsp. chopped parsley
3 Tbsp. olive oil
1 clove garlic, minced
1½ Tbsp. red wine vinegar
½ tsp. soy sauce
Salt and pepper to taste
1 pita, halved

Combine ingredients. Chill. Fill pockets just before serving.

HAM-POTATO SALAD FILLING (6 servings)

3 cups cooked, diced potatoes
2 cups cooked, diced ham
3 hard-cooked eggs, chopped
½ cup shredded Cheddar cheese
¼ cup chopped green onion
¾ cup mayonnaise
1 Tbsp. Worcestershire sauce
¼ tsp. pepper
¼ tsp. wine vinegar
3 pitas, halved

Combine potatoes, ham, eggs, and cheese. Toss lightly to mix well.

In bowl, combine mayonnaise, Worcestershire, onion, pepper, and vinegar. Mix with potato-ham mixture. Spoon mixture into pockets just before serving.

HOLIDAY LEFTOVERS IN A POCKET

Thinly sliced turkey
Leftover stuffing
Cranberry sauce
Mayonnaise
Pitas, halved

Spread mayonnaise on the insides of pockets. Add turkey and stuffing. Top with a spoonful of cranberry sauce.

LAMB MEATLOAF IN A PITA (6 servings)

¾ lb. lean ground lamb
1 egg, beaten
2 Tbsp. minced onion
1 Tbsp. minced green pepper
1 tsp. minced garlic
¼ cup whole kernel corn
⅓ cup diced tomatoes
½ tsp. dried oregano leaves
3 Tbsp. wheat germ
¼ tsp. salt
¼ tsp. pepper
3 pitas, halved
Yogurt

Combine all ingredients, except pitas and yogurt. Form into loaf and bake at 350°F. 1 hour. Cool. Chill.

Spread yogurt on inside of pita pockets. Fill pockets with chilled meat and top filling with additional yogurt.

MARINATED BEEF AND VEGETABLE FILLING (6 servings)

1 lb. top round steak, cut into thin strips
1 tsp. salt
⅓ cup olive oil
1 large onion, sliced
½ lb. Chinese pea pods
1 can garbanzo beans, drained
⅓ cup wine vinegar
1½ tsp. sugar
½ tsp. thyme leaves
½ tsp. dry mustard
3 drops hot pepper sauce
¼ tsp. pepper
3 pitas, halved

Saute´ onion in ¼ cup olive oil. Add pea pods and cook 3 minutes. Remove vegetables from oil and set aside.
In oil, brown meat which has been mixed with salt. Add meat to vegetables. Stir in remaining oil, garbanzo beans, vinegar, sugar, thyme, mustard, hot pepper sauce, and pepper. Toss well. Cover and chill 2 to 3 hours. Fill pockets with mixture at serving time.

ORIENTAL SHRIMP SALAD FILLING (6 servings)

2 cups cooked rice
3 Tbsp. grated onion
1 Tbsp. grated lemon rind
⅔ cup mayonnaise
1 Tbsp. lemon juice
1 tsp. soy sauce
1 Tbsp. Worcestershire sauce
Dash hot pepper sauce
¾ lb. cooked deveined shrimp
6 hard-cooked eggs, chopped
3 pitas, halved

Combine all ingredients, except pita, and mix well. Chill. Spoon mixture into pockets at serving time.

PHILADELPHIA FILLING (4 servings)

¼ cup olive oil
24 thin slices salami
16 thin slices Provalone cheese
16 thin slices Capocollo
1 cup shredded lettuce
½ cup chopped sweet onion
8 slices tomato
12 hot cherry peppers, halved and seeded
2 pitas, halved

Brush insides of pockets with olive oil, then start stuffing!

PINEAPPLE-SHRIMP SALAD FILLING (6 servings)

3 5-oz. cans drained shrimp
2 cups drained pineapple chunks
2 oranges, peeled and sectioned
1 avocado, diced
2 Tbsp. lemon juice
2 Tbsp. dry white wine
1 tsp. honey
¼ tsp. salt
½ tsp. paprika
½ cup olive oil
3 pita, halved

Combine shrimp, pineapple, oranges, avocado, and lemon juice. Chill.
Mix together wine, honey, salt, paprika, and olive oil. Pour over chilled ingredients. Spoon into pockets just before serving.

ROAST BEEF SALAD FILLING (4 servings)

2 cups diced cooked roast beef
1/2 cup diced cooked potatoes
1/2 cup diced cooked carrots
1/2 cup mayonnaise
2 hard-cooked eggs, diced
1 medium onion, minced
1/2 cup chopped sweet pickle
Salt and pepper to taste
2 pitas, halved
Mayonnaise

Combine ingredients, except pita, and toss well. Chill. Spread mayonnaise on insides of pockets, then fill with meat mixture.

ROAST BEEF SUPREME (4 servings)

1/2 cup mango chutney
1/2 lb. thinly sliced, cooked roast beef
1 large Spanish onion, sliced
1 medium cucumber, sliced
1 red pepper, thinly sliced
2 pitas, halved
Sour cream

Spread insides of pockets with chutney. Add beef, onion, cucumber, and red pepper. Top filling with sour cream.

SAN MARINO BEEF FILLING (4 servings)

3 cups medium-well roast,
    cut into julienne strips
1 medium red onion,
    sliced into rings and separated
3 medium carrots,
    cut into julienne strips
3 stalks celery,
    cut into julienne strips
2 green peppers,
    cut into julienne strips
1/2 cup grated carrot
1/2 cup grated onion
1/4 cup olive oil
1/4 cup red wine vinegar
1/2 tsp. dry mustard
1/2 tsp. salt
Dash hot pepper sauce
2 pitas, halved

Combine beef, onion rings, and the carrot, celery, and green pepper strips in bowl. Chill. Combine remaining ingredients, except pita; mix well. Chill.

At serving time, toss meat and vegetables with 1/4 cup dressing and spoon into pockets. Serve with additional dressing.

SARDINE FILLING (4 servings)

1/4 cup mayonnaise
1 tsp. paprika
6 slices American cheese, cut into strips
2 tomatoes, sliced
Shredded lettuce
20 canned sardines
Salt and pepper to taste
2 pitas, halved

Mix together mayonnaise and paprika; spread on insides of pockets. Fill pockets with remaining ingredients.

SHRIMP AVOCADO FILLING (8 servings)

3 avocados, peeled, pitted, and diced
1 lb. cooked shrimp, deveined and chopped
1 medium onion, chopped
¼ cup oil
2 Tbsp. vinegar
½ garlic clove, crushed
¼ tsp. dry mustard
¼ tsp. salt
¼ tsp. pepper
4 pitas, halved

Combine shrimp, avocado, and onion. Set aside.
Mix together oil, vinegar, garlic, mustard, salt, and pepper. Toss dressing with avocado mixture. Fill pockets with filling.

TAHITIAN SALAD FILLING (6 servings)

1 cup diced crab meat
1 cup diced orange sections
3 ripe mangoes, diced
3 bananas, diced
1 8-oz. can pineapple chunks, drained
½ cup shredded coconut
½ cup chopped pecans
3 Tbsp. sugar
½ cup freshly squeezed lemon juice
3 pitas, halved

Combine all ingredients, except pita. Chill. Spoon filling into pockets and serve at once.

TUNA-EGG SALAD FILLING (2 servings)

1 cup canned tuna
2 hard-cooked eggs, chopped
2 Tbsp. minced parsley
1 Tbsp. minced onion
½ cup chopped celery
1 apple, grated
2 Tbsp. horseradish
2 Tbsp. mayonnaise
Salt and pepper to taste
1 pita, halved

Combine all ingredients, except pita, and mix thoroughly. Chill. Fill pockets with mixture just before serving time.

TUNA-FRUIT SALAD FILLING (6 servings)

2 7-oz. cans tuna, drained and flaked
1 cup diced apples
½ cup diced celery
½ cup chopped cashews
½ cup mayonnaise
½ cup crumbled Blue cheese
3 pitas, halved

Combine all ingredients, except pita. Chill. Spoon into pockets and serve at once.

TURKEY SALAD FILLING (2 servings)

2 cups minced cooked turkey
¼ cup minced celery
2 Tbsp. chopped pimiento
2 Tbsp. sauterne
¼ cup mayonnaise
¼ tsp. salt
Dash pepper
1 pita, halved

Combine turkey, celery, pimiento, wine, mayonnaise, and seasonings. Chill. Fill pockets at serving time.

VAMPIRE SUPREME (8 servings)

3 lbs. top sirloin, all visible fat removed
2 egg yolks
½ cup finely grated Bermuda onion
4 capers, crushed
1 mashed anchovy
½ cup finely minced parsley
4 pitas, halved

With the back of a knife scrape the steak, turning the meat several times until only the fiber remains. Discard fibers (or feed them to the cat). Add yolks, onion, capers, anchovy, and parsley to scraped meat. Mix well. Fill pockets with mixture.

Chapter 11

More Hot Fillings

BAJA CHICKEN FILLING (8 servings)

    4 boned chicken breasts, skinned and split in half
    Seasoned salt
    Pepper
    6 Tbsp. cooking oil
    3 cloves garlic, crushed
    ¼ cup tarragon vinegar
    ⅔ cup dry sherry
    4 pitas, halved
    Sour cream

    Sprinkle chicken with salt and pepper. Combine garlic with oil and vinegar in frying pan. Sauté chicken in oil until browned. Remove from pan and place in baking dish. Sprinkle with sherry and bake 350°F. for 15 minutes. Place half breast in each pocket and top with sour cream.

B-B-QUED PORK FILLING (6 servings)

    4 lb. pork roast
    1 large diced onion
    1 can (6-oz.) tomato paste
    ¾ cup water
    1 cup tomato juice
    ½ cup brown sugar

3 Tbsp. vinegar
2 Tbsp. Worcestershire sauce
1 tsp. salt
1 tsp. pepper
½ tsp. chili powder
½ tsp. cinnamon
¼ tsp. ground cloves
3 pitas, halved

Cook and shred roast. Set aside.

Combine remaining ingredients (except pita) and simmer 15 to 20 minutes. Add meat and simmer 15 minutes longer. Spoon filling into pockets and serve at once.

BEEF BARBECUE FILLING (16 servings)

2 Tbsp. butter
1 medium-sized onion, chopped
1 garlic clove, minced
½ cup celery, chopped
¾ cup water
1 cup catsup
2 Tbsp. lemon juice
2 Tbsp. Worcestershire sauce
2 Tbsp. brown sugar
1 Tbsp. vinegar
1 tsp. dry mustard
¼ tsp. salt
¼ tsp. pepper
3 lbs. cooked roast beef, thinly sliced
8 pitas, halved

Sauté onion, garlic, and celery in butter. Add remaining ingredients, except roast and pita, and simmer 20 minutes.

Place beef in baking pan and cover with sauce. Bake in 350°F. oven 30 minutes. Spoon mixture into heated pockets.

BEEF TERIYAKI FILLING (6 servings)

⅔ cup soy sauce
¼ cup dry sherry
2 Tbsp. sugar
1 tsp. ground ginger
2 cloves garlic, minced
2 lbs. beef sirloin steak,
  cut into julienne strips
3 pitas, halved

Combine first 5 ingredients in baking pan. Add meat; cover and marinate at room temperature 2 hours. Remove meat from marinade and stir fry in skillet to desired doneness. Spoon into pockets and add a dash of marinade, if desired. Serve at once.

CHEESY HASH FILLING (4 servings)

¾ cup shredded Cheddar cheese
1 small can corned beef hash
1 Tbsp. mustard with horseradish
2 Tbsp. Worcestershire
2 pitas, halved

Combine cheese, hash, mustard, and Worcestershire sauce in saucepan. Heat thoroughly, spoon into pockets and serve at once.

CHILI BURGER FILLING (6 servings)

1 lb. ground beef
1 cup chopped onion
2 cloves garlic, minced
1 16-oz. can tomatoes, drained and chopped
1 6-oz. can tomato paste
¼ cup chopped green pepper
1 tsp. seasoned salt
1 tsp. chili powder

¼ tsp. dried oregano, crushed
Parmesan cheese
3 pitas, halved

Brown beef, onion, and garlic in skillet. Drain off fat. Stir in tomatoes, tomato paste, green pepper, and seasonings. Simmer, covered, 15 minutes.
Spoon filling into pockets and top with grated Parmesan cheese.

CURRIED EGG FILLING (6 servings)

1 medium onion, minced
1 clove garlic, minced
½ small ginger root, grated
1½ Tbsp. butter
½ Tbsp. curry powder
1½ Tbsp. flour
1 cup chicken bouillon
1½ cups evaporated milk
1 cup raisins
¼ cup dried apples, diced
2 Tbsp. lemon juice
¼ tsp. salt
8 hard-cooked eggs
3 pitas, halved

Sauté onion, garlic, and ginger in butter until lightly browned. Stir in curry powder and flour. Heat together bouillon and milk, then gradually stir into flour-butter mixture. Stir and simmer until smooth. Add raisins, apple, and lemon juice. Season with salt. Peel and slice eggs and add to sauce. Spoon filling into pockets.

CURRIED LAMB FILLING (8 servings)

2 lbs. boneless lamb, cubed
2 Tbsp. olive oil
1½ cups water
1 medium-sized onion, sliced
1 tsp. salt
¼ tsp. pepper
1 bay leaf
¼ cup flour
2 tsp. curry powder
1 Tbsp. snipped parsley
4 pitas, halved
Raisins
Peanuts
Flaked coconut
Chutney

Brown meat in oil. Add water, onion, salt, pepper, and bay leaf. Cover and cook slowly for 1½ hours. Remove bay leaf.

Mix flour and curry powder with ¼ cup water, then stir into hot meat mixture and cook until mixture thickens; add parsley.

Spoon into pockets and top with raisins, peanuts, coconut, and chutney.

CURRIED TURKEY FILLING (8 servings)

¼ cup butter
3 tsp. curry powder
½ cup chopped onion
3 Tbsp. flour
Dash salt and pepper
1½ cups chicken broth
2½ cups diced cooked turkey
1½ tsp. grated lemon peel
½ cup chopped cashew nuts
4 pitas, halved

Melt butter in medium-sized skillet. Add curry and heat 2 to 3 minutes. Stir in onion and cook until tender. Blend in flour and seasoning. Add broth all at once and cook and stir until boiling. Reduce heat and simmer 3 minutes. Add turkey, lemon peeling, and cashews. Heat thoroughly. Spoon into pockets and serve at once.

EMPANADA FILLING (2 servings)

⅓ cup raisins
½ small onion, minced
1 clove garlic, minced
½ lb. lean ground beef
¼ cup olive oil
1 tsp. flour
¼ cup beef broth or bouillon
12 pitted green olives, chopped
Dash pepper
1 pita, halved

Soak raisins in boiling water ½ hour. Drain well. Sauté onion, garlic, and beef in hot olive oil. Add flour and brown slightly. Add remaining ingredients and heat through. Fill pockets and serve immediately.

HOT CRAB FILLING (6 servings)

2 cups cooked crab meat
¼ cup mayonnaise
1 3-oz. pkg. cream cheese, softened
2 egg yolks
2 tsp. finely chopped onion
½ tsp. prepared mustard
3 pitas, halved
Butter

Butter insides of pockets. Combine crab meat with mayonnaise. Divide crab meat among pockets.
Mix together cream cheese, egg yolks, onion, and mustard. Spoon over crab in pockets. Broil in oven until filling is bubbly and golden.

HOT SLAW FILLING (4 servings)

3 eggs, beaten
1/3 cup water
1/4 cup vinegar
1/4 tsp. salt
2 tsp. prepared mustard
3 Tbsp. sugar
1 tsp. caraway seeds
2 Tbsp. butter
1 1/2 pt. shredded cabbage
2 pitas, halved

Combine eggs, water, vinegar, salt, mustard, sugar, and caraway seeds in saucepan. Cook, stirring frequently, until thick. Add butter and cabbage to seed mixture, mixing thoroughly. Cover and cook 15 minutes. Spoon into heated pockets.

HOT TURKEY-RELISH FILLING (4 servings)

2 cups cooked turkey, diced
1/2 cup celery, finely chopped
2/3 cup cranberry-orange relish
1/2 cup mayonnaise
2 pitas, halved

Combine turkey, celery, relish, and mayonnaise in bowl. Spoon into pockets and wrap each pocket in foil. Heat in 350°F. oven 15 minutes.

LEBANESE LAMB FILLING (2 servings)

¼ cup butter
2 cups finely ground lamb
1 egg, beaten
¼ tsp. salt
¼ tsp. each nutmeg, cinnamon, allspice
1 Tbsp. milk
1 cup cooked rice
1 pita, halved

Cook egg and lamb in butter until meat is browned. Add salt, spices, milk, and rice. Heat through. Fill pockets and serve at once. (May be topped with a spoonful of yogurt or sour cream.)

ORIENTAL SHRIMP FILLING (4 servings)

2 Tbsp. peanut oil
2 Tbsp. green onion, minced
1 cup celery, minced
3 cups mung bean sprouts
1 can (4½ oz.) shrimp, drained
1 Tbsp. soy sauce
1 Tbsp. cooking sherry
1 egg
2 Tbsp. water
1 Tbsp. cornstarch
2 pitas, halved

Heat oil in skillet, sauté onions and celery. Add sprouts, shrimp, soy sauce, and sherry; heat. Beat egg slightly with water; mix in cornstarch and blend until smooth. Add cornstarch mixture to heated ingredients in pan. Bring to boiling and cook until thick. Spoon into pockets and serve with additional soy sauce.

PIZZA BURGER FILLING (4 servings)

1 cup tomato sauce
1 tsp. oregano
½ tsp. basil
¼ tsp. garlic powder
1 lb. ground beef
¼ cup bread crumbs
¼ cup grated Parmesan cheese
1 egg, beaten
4 slices Mozzarella cheese
2 pitas, halved

Combine tomato sauce with herbs and garlic powder in saucepan. Bring to boiling; reduce heat and simmer gently while preparing burgers.

Mix beef with bread crumbs, Parmesan, and egg. Shape into 4 patties and broil, turning once, until almost done. Top each with a slice of Mozzarella cheese. Continue to broil until cheese is melted. Place burgers in pita pockets and spoon sauce over. Serve at once.

SPANISH LAMB FILLING (8 servings)

½ cup finely chopped onion
1 clove garlic, minced
1 Tbsp. cooking oil
1 20-oz. can tomatoes, drained and chopped
1 8-oz. can tomato sauce
1½ cups sliced mushrooms
1 tsp. basil
2 cups sliced pimiento-stuffed olives
2 cups diced cooked lamb
¼ cup sliced pimiento-stuffed olives
4 pitas, halved

In saucepan, cook onion and garlic in oil until tender. Stir in tomatoes, tomato sauce, mushrooms, and basil. Simmer, covered, 1 hour. Uncover and simmer 30 minutes longer, stirring occasionally. Stir in lamb and olives; simmer 10 minutes. Fill pockets just before serving.

WILTED SPINACH WITH LIVER AND BACON (6 servings)

1 10-oz. bag spinach, torn into bite-sized pieces
1 lb. chicken livers, chopped
6 slices bacon, diced
1 small onion, chopped
¼ cup water
¼ cup fresh lemon juice
3 Tbsp. cider vinegar
½ tsp. salt
½ tsp. mustard
3 pitas, halved

Cook bacon until crisp. Remove from skillet. Cook liver and onion in drippings in skillet until liver is browned. Add water, lemon juice, vinegar, mustard and salt; heat to boiling. Pour over spinach. Toss well. Spoon into pockets and sprinkle filling with bacon.

INDEX

Appetizers   Page
Cheese
Beer-Cheese Filling 84
Cheese-Curry Filling 85
Cheese-Supreme Filling 85
Chili Con Questa 85
Eggs
Olive-Egg Filling 89
Fish
Avocado-Salmon Filling 83
Fishy-Onion Filling 87
Herring in Sour Cream Filling 87
Salmon Filling 89
Smoked Fish Filling 90
Liver
Liver Filling 88
Pork
Deviled Ham Filling 86
New Zealand Filling 89
Seafoods
Clam and Cheese Filling 84
Crabmeat Filling 86
Seafood Filling 90
Vegetables
Black Olive Pate' Filling 84
Guacamole 87
Mushroom Filling 88
Turkish Eggplant Filling 91

Beef

Corned Beef
Cheesy Hash Filling 118
Corned Beef Supreme 28
Red Flannel Hash in Rye 30
Reuben Pocket 31

Ground Beef
Burger Oriental Filling 74
Chili Burger in a Cornmeal Pocket 16
Chili Burger Filling 118
Empanada Filling 121
Greek Beef Pockets 7
Meatballs Italiano in Pockets 56
Papa Joe's Pita 57
Pita Enchilada 18
Pita With Parmesan Patties 10
Pizza Burger Filling 124
Pocket Full of Chili 19
Pocket of Meatloaf 11
Sesame Pita Cheese Burger 44
Sloppy Joes in Pita 13
Sour Cream Pita Burgers 60
South of the Border Pockets 21
Swedish Meatballs in Rye 33
Sweet and Sour Meatball Filling 44
Taco in a Pocket 22
Tamale Filling 23

Roast Beef
Beef-Bacon Scramble in a Pita 26
Beef Barbecue Filling 117
Beef-Raisin Filling 15
Hash in a Pocket 7
Meat 'N Potatoes in Pockets 78
Pocket with Hash Filling 20
Roast Beef Pita Boy 31
Roast Beef Salad Filling 111
Roast Beef Supreme 111
San Marino Beef Filling 112

Steak
- Austrian Beef Filling ... 4
- Beef Burgundy Filling ... 26
- Beef Burma in Whole Wheat ... 74
- Beef Strips, Belgium Style ... 63
- Beef Stroganoff Filling ... 27
- Beef Teriyaki Filling ... 118
- Beef Zinger ... 64
- Brochetts ... 64
- French Tenderloin Filling ... 6
- Hot Ginger Steak Filling ... 76
- Italian Cube Steaks in Pita ... 77
- Polynesian Beef Filling ... 59
- The Red Baron ... 80
- Sesame Full of Chop Suey ... 43
- Shish Kabobs in Pita ... 80
- Sirloin-Mushroom Filling ... 59
- West Indies Steak Filling ... 70
- Vampire Supreme ... 115

Veal
- Dilled Veal Filling ... 66
- Latvia Filling ... 67
- Sweet-Sour Veal Filling ... 13
- Veal-Oyster Loaf Filling ... 82

Breads
- Basic Pita ... 3
- Cornmeal Pita ... 14
- Dessert Pita ... 92
- Honey-Cracked Wheat Pita ... 73
- Rye Pita ... 24
- Sesame Pita ... 34
- Sourdough Pita ... 50
- Triticale Pita ... 62
- Whole Wheat Pita ... 72
- Whole Wheat Sourdough Pita ... 50

Cheese
Avocado-Swiss Filling 25
California Energy Filling 15
Pocket Nacho 20

Desserts
Chiffons
Coconut Chiffon Filling 94
Strawberry Chiffon Filling 102
Cream Filling
Creamy Banana Filling 95
Easy Lemon Filling 95
Lemon-Cheese Filling 97
Mocha Chocolate Cream Filling 97
Peach Cream Filling 98
Pineapple Cream Filling 100
Custard Filling
Caramel Flan in a Pocket 93
Pecan Filling 99
Pumpkin Custard Filling 101
Fruit Filling
Apple-Mince Filling 93
Cherry Filling 94
Fresh Apricot Filling 96
Fresh Plum Filling 96
Pear Crumble Filling 99
Pocket Strawberry Short Cake 100
Quick Apple-Cheese Filling 103
Rhubarb Filling 101
Spiced Apple Filling 102
Strawberry-Rhubarb Filling 103

Eggs
Curried Egg Filling 119
Eggs, Country Style 29
Huevos Espanol en un Bolsillo 18
Oriental Scramble in a Pita 9
Pocket of Egg Foo Yung 42
Western Style Eggs in Pita 61

Fish
Cod
Codfish Hash in Rye 28
Fillets
Flounder in a Pocket 17
Pocket Fishwich 58
Pocket of Sole, Polynesian Style 43
Herring
Herring in Sourdough 57
Salmon
Alaskan Pocket Breakfast 51
Poached Salmon in Pita 11
Salmon-Pineapple Filling 32
Salmon-Tomato Filling 12
Sardine
Sardine Filling 112
Tuna
Artichoke-Tuna Filling 63
Tuna-Chutney-Cheese Filling 33
Tuna-Egg Salad Filling 114
Tuna Patties in Sesame 45
Tuna Sprout Pocket Salad 81
Whitefish
Smoked Whitefish and Cream Cheese 60

Frankfurters
Franks Ole' 17
Frank in a Pocket 6
Hot Dogs with Chili Beef Sauce 8
Pocket Franks and Beans 78
Pita Kraut Dog 10

Lamb
Chops
Turkish Lamb Filling 82
Precooked
Chilled Lamb Filling 105
East Indian Lamb Filling 75

Lamb and Marinated Onions in Sesame 39
Spanish Lamb Filling 124
Cubed
Curried Lamb Filling 120
Garlic Lamb Kabobs in a Pocket 66
Hawaiian Lamb Filling 39
Lamb Kabobs in Sourdough 55
Ground
Chili Lamb Filling 36
Greek Gyros 75
Lamb Meatloaf in Pita 108
Lebanese Lamb Filling 123
Minted Lamb Patties in Pockets 68
Turkish Lamb Filling 82

Liver
Beef
Rye Filled With Liver and Onions 31
Chicken
Chicken Livers Supreme 36
Deviled Chicken Livers in Pockets 5
Rumaki in Pita 79
Wilted Spinach with Liver and Bacon 125

Pork
Precooked
Polish Peasant Pockets 79
Ground
Pork and Apple Patties in Cornmeal 21
Ham
Avocado-Ham Scramble 4
Club in a Pita 65
Ham Patties with Cherry Sauce 54
Ham-Potato Salad Filling 107
Ham and Swiss in Rye 30
Roast
B-B-Qued Pork Filling 116

Shoulder
  Chinese Pork Filling 37
  Green Beans and Pork in a Pocket 38
  Sweet and Sour Pork Filling 60

Poultry
Chicken
  Baja Chicken Filling 116
  Chick-a-pita 35
  Chinese Chicken Salad Filling 104
  Creamed Chicken and Ham Filling 52
  Fruited Chicken Filling 106
  Oriental Chicken Filling 40
  Pineapple Chicken Salad Pita 41
Turkey
  Curried Turkey Filling 120
  Flaming Turkey Pockets 53
  Holiday Leftovers in a Pocket 108
  Hot Turkey Relish Filling 122
  Turkey Salad Filling 115

Sausage
  Baked Brauschweiger Filling 25
  Chorizo-Frijole Filling 16
  Flying Saucers 53
  German Potato Salad Filling 67
  Knackwurst-Swiss Pita Melt 30
  Lasagna in Sourdough 55
  Philadelphia Filling 110
  Pita with Italian Sausages 58
  Pocket of Pizza 12
  Sausage-Apple Filling 69

Seafood
Clams
  Clam Fritters in Triticale 65
  Steamed Clams in a Pocket 81

Crab
   Artichoke-Crab Filling 51
   Crab Cakes in Pockets 37
   Hot Crab Filling 121
   Pocket Crab Salad 42
   Tahitian Salad Filling 113
Lobster
   Lobster Salad Pocket 8
Oysters
   Oyster Loaf in Sesame 41
   Veal-Oyster Loaf 82
Scallops
   Curried Seafood in Sourdough 52
   Oriental Shrimp Filling 123
   Oriental Shrimp Salad Filling 109
   Pineapple-Shrimp Salad Filling 110
   Shrimp-Avocado Filling 113

Vegetables
   Artichokes Vinaigrette in Pita 73
   Avocado Salad in a Pita 5
   Bean Salad Filling 104
   Eggplant Salad Filling 105
   Falafel in Rye Pocket 29
   Garbanzo and Mushroom Filling 107
   Hot Slaw Filling 122
   Italian Eggplant Filling 77
   Pita Bean Burritos 9
   Soybean Filling 32
   Tabuli in Pocket 70